the life of
total
ootball

the life of
total
football

The Origins and Development of
Football's Most Entertaining Philosophy

James Jackson

First published by Pitch Publishing, 2024

Pitch Publishing
9 Donnington Park,
85 Birdham Road,
Chichester,
West Sussex,
PO20 7AJ
www.pitchpublishing.co.uk
info@pitchpublishing.co.uk

A CIP catalogue record is available for this book
from the British Library.

ISBN 978 1 80150 189 7

Typesetting and origination by Pitch Publishing
Printed and bound in India by Thomson Press

Contents

This book has been a pleasure to create. I hope I have done the game of football – and Total Football – justice. Thank you to my wife and family, Rachel, Ella and Alma. This book would never have been possible without my father's inspiration. A special mention to Noah, Jamie and Archie, who will one day play the game like the names mentioned within. And I can't forget Ruth!

Introduction

IN 2003, I was in my early teens and I shared an obsession with football with the friends with whom I played the gamr every single night of the week. I recall feeling great anguish at having been just too young to enjoy the glory days of the team I support, Newcastle United, under Kevin Keegan. Looking back now, I can see I was spoilt in comparison to younger NUFC fans (before the recent takeover, of course). I'm sure fans of many clubs around the world can relate to this, the feeling that something is missing. Football changes, great teams fall, others rise. But it is not just great footballing minds that can propel teams to the top. Money plays a bigger role than ever. Growing up supporting a team managed by Sir Bobby Robson, I was spoilt rotten. He was one of the greatest English managers and certainly the easiest to adore.

Like any young fan, my love of football was largely influenced – and blinded – by the commercialisation of the game. I would rarely fully concentrate on a match, my attention flicking in and out. The boots the players wore or their goal celebrations were what really mattered to me. My views on the game were often just me echoing those of my brother and father. What they were shouting at the TV often seemed to be the opposite of what the pundits were saying, but I would automatically take their side rather than reaching my own conclusions. That was the case until I watched the most skilful player I had ever seen – Ronaldo de Assis Moreira, more commonly known as Ronaldinho. I began to piece together what made me love the game. Suddenly, it all made more sense. My love for Total Football was ignited.

In my house, there was football on all the time, although my father, Robin, never pressured me into playing or watching. Looking back, he has been the main influence on my relationship with football. It was as if he had buried it in my psyche and the spark just needed to catch alight. Our annual holidays in Europe would always end up football-related – to my mother's delight, I'm sure! Vivid memories include taking the excellent Amsterdam ArenA tour and cycling for miles to find a Dutch village where Barcelona were holding their pre-season training camp (we were refused entry to the facility, but we could just about make out a few players going through some drills). Another year, we even attended a Newcastle pre-season game against a Dutch non-league side. As a child, I knew all the top European players, mainly from the computer game Pro Evolution Soccer. To reiterate, my early outlook on the game was hugely influenced by commercials and PlayStation. However, my true beliefs lay deeper and the way I looked at football changed one night while watching a Barcelona match. I was mesmerised by their style of play and this proved to be the ignition inside my brain, the trigger.

After that, I would listen out for the voice of former Northern Ireland striker Gerry Armstrong, the expert summariser for Sky Sports' coverage of La Liga, drifting up from the TV downstairs and, if Barcelona were playing, I would abandon my PlayStation. I started to really enjoy watching the games. My father would pass comments on what was good or bad and we would end up discussing all things football. The same names would always pop up. What Ronaldinho did during those early seasons at Barcelona was remarkable. I would often claim he was the greatest player ever, to which my father would laugh and tell me: 'Don't be daft.' I would always ask him: 'Who *was* the greatest ever then?' I had heard of the usual suspects – Pelé, Diego Maradona, George Best. He, though, would discount these names, saying something like: 'Well, everyone says one of them lot. However, for me, the greatest player I have ever seen and will ever see was a man called Johan Cruyff.' This would later be proven wrong by Lionel Messi.

My father, born in the Scottish Borders, grew up in the fishing town of Eyemouth. Playing football – not only on the streets and fields, but on the beach – is a memory he holds very close. He grew up following the infamous wave of 1960s and 1970s mavericks who graced Scottish football and Willie Hamilton was my dad's idol. However, it was a similar experience to mine that hatched his love for the game. In the 1960 European Cup Final, Real Madrid took on Eintracht Frankfurt at Hampden. A record crowd of 127,621 packed into the ground and every single one of them left the stadium drooling with amazement at the Spanish side. The Madrid team was packed with superstars – Ferenc Puskás, Alfredo di Stefano, Luis del Sol, Paco Gento and Jose Santamaria.

It was their style of play that astonished everyone, including teenagers Alex Ferguson and Billy McNeill, who were in the crowd along with many other soon-to-be legends of the British game. For my father, he watched it from the comfort of his own home, as this was the first televised European game he can remember, and the experience has never left him. Even more than 60 years later, when I ask him to recall that game, his eyes light up. 'I remember watching it and saying "Wow, this is what football is."' The game the British exported in the early 1900s had returned 50 years later and the fact it returned to Scotland is even more precious, as we will find out. Most importantly, though, it had returned as a totally different beast. What the hell had happened? As when the Hungarians humbled England in 1953, this game was another wake-up call for British football, evidence it was being left behind at its own game. After falling in love with what he had seen, my dad frantically tried to follow up on it and the work of journalists Hugh McIlvanney and Brian Granville made this easier. They critiqued the game in the manner my father was looking for, covering more of the international game.

Football had developed so much in half a century that the British, once pioneers who taught the game abroad, now needed to reverse the cycle, seeking foreigners to bring the game back to the island on which it was created. They had to teach themselves football again. But did they listen?

My interest in Total Football really took off by watching Barcelona, and all those subtle clues from my early childhood would be triggered. Having listened to my dad's stories of the great Dutch team of the 1974 World Cup and the legendary Hungarians of the 1950s, I want this book to not only capture the essence of what Total Football is but why it has impacted the world of football the way it has. For me, the facts that surround football are far removed from the actual reason we love the game. By facts, I am mainly speaking about stats and trophies.

Take, for example, Real Madrid's most recent hat-trick of Champions League triumphs. No one will convince me that that Real Madrid team, based on their style of play or even the great victories they achieved, come anywhere near the Ajax team which scored a hat-trick of European Cup triumphs in the 1970s. But there it is, written into the history books, and, to some people, points or trophies are more than enough to label a team 'great'. I understand that the ultimate aim of the game is to win, I do appreciate there are many different styles of play and I realise that, frankly, my opinion means absolutely nothing. I have seen enough football at a decent level to understand that the game isn't always pretty. I join the NUFC roller coaster every matchday, riding on excitement and my pride that I support the greatest club in the world, but reality slaps me in the face every game, about 15 minutes in. But when we win? My head goes and I have somehow tricked myself again, believing that we are the greatest.

Football drags you in, that's why we love it. However, when I sit down and think about how I would really want my team to play, it would be Total Football. Now, this is not to belittle what teams have achieved using different styles, because if everyone played the same way … well, actually, if everyone *did* play Total Football, it would be quite fascinating! But you understand what I'm saying. Teams win trophies by being the best side in a competition and it is a fantastic achievement, but our love for the modern game is fading, without us even noticing.

Winning has become everything and the teams who don't win multiple trophies don't last long at the top or even in people's memories. However, the teams captured in this book will never leave the minds of those who hear their stories. Which is why it's so important to include some of the early developments in football which have a clear link to what Rinus Michels created with his Ajax team in the late 1960s. Total Football wasn't really heard of until the Netherlands national team's performances at the 1974 World Cup. It is a tournament they didn't even win, yet that team are still rightfully celebrated half a century later. But the roots of Total Football came from before Michels was even born. As all football theories and tactics have the same goal – to win – why did Michels use the tools left for him by the names you'll hear in the early chapters of this book? Can Total Football still be used now? To inspire, to entertain, to develop players and win matches?

As I began to write this book, we had just endured almost two full seasons of games being played behind closed doors, with multiple games on the TV almost every day. Did we watch these games? Of course. But did we actually watch them and enjoy them like we used to? For me, watching football became something of a chore in 2020 and 2021. These days, you never miss anything. Highlights, goals and analysis are uploaded online in an instant and, before you even have time to process the game, another teamsheet is released and the process starts all over again. Mass-produced football suits certain faculties of the game, usually the ones with the motivation of making money. However, it also has to be seen as a plus for the fans, as we never miss a kick. Without widespread TV coverage in the 1960s and 1970s, fans would only catch brief glimpses of other teams unless they attended games in person.

Is this a reason why teams were allowed longer to implement styles of play back then, as they would not be scrutinised as much as teams who don't deliver success instantly are now? The link between fanbase and club owners is drifting and breaking as seasons go by, meaning that, even if fans don't mind sacrificing trophies in return for entertaining football, this is often overlooked by the business people in charge of the clubs. We must not flush football theories away from the game completely. I hope to capture what Total Football is, to make sure we understand the benefits of using it. As we gradually lose the game to the business world, will it be yet another art thrown into the fire of money-making over quality? There comes a time when we must ask ourselves, is this business or art? Or is it nothing but a game of football?

A simplified look at Total Football is commonly summed up in a short paragraph, so what's the need for a book on it? Remarkably, without any direct links, Rinus Michels and Valeriy Lobanovskyi both came to the same conclusion almost simultaneously in the 1970s, that football was all about space. Michels is the name most commonly associated with Total Football. Lobanovskyi, however, was implementing similar ideas with his Dynamo Kyiv side as Michels was with the Dutch national team.[1] This, I feel, was nothing more than a remarkable coincidence. Rather than taking inspiration from one another, they created the style of play at around the same time. This, to me, proves that their knowledge was based on foundations laid long before they started coaching.

Their beliefs were dominated by the use of space, with the following points being the membrane of a theory I will look at in more depth:

- Make the pitch big when you have possession, making it easier to retain the ball.
- Make the pitch smaller when you don't have possession, making it harder for the opposition to retain possession.
- Encourage players to interchange positions.

- Rely on players to cover for each other.
- Use an aggressive offside trap.
- Press opponents and engage the ball when out of possession.
- Move the ball quickly and constantly when in possession.

Finding out what Total Football is and why it was implemented can only really be achieved by looking at how Total Football came about. If it was as easy as simply relaying the key points and people understanding them sufficiently to implement them on the field, football would be a much easier game to understand; but a lot less fascinating. I want to tell the whole story; how all the experiences of the people I will mention interlock, through wars, uprisings, different highs and lows. Most of the time, it would be luck or fate that brought these characters together.

It is a tale which starts with a Scotsman and travels through Hungary, Austria, South America and Holland and spreads to the rest of the world. We will look at how close Total Football was to being built into the British football foundations, only for the English to reject the opportunity on several occasions, inadvertently leading to that knowledge being implemented overseas instead. What happened after the devastating defeat for the Dutch at the 1974 World Cup and how did they get to the final in the first place? The story will hopefully inspire you, if you do not already, to believe in this philosophy and fall in love with this side of the game.

It has given me so much joy and continues to help salvage my slowly fading love of the modern game. Although parts of the story will have no direct link to Total Football, especially the tales before Michels created it, I feel this is part of the quest. To draw up the life of Total Football is vital, as everything in life needs a steady foundation to withstand the test of time. Arsène Wenger, reflecting on his development as a coach, once said he always admired coaches like Johan Cruyff who made their team play first and did not just count on their opponents' weaknesses; to Wenger 'football can only call itself a profession if its aim is to make people dream. I understood this as I watched those men coach their teams.' [2]

Total Football, I believe, stretches much further than the 90 minutes of a match. Those who have believed in it and followed it often also seem to be outstanding role models and leaders. Their thoughts often become priceless anecdotes that you can use in other aspects of life, not just football. Some people choose to highlight Cruyff's sometimes confrontational personality; how he sometimes didn't have much patience for those who did not follow the same beliefs as him and how he always ensured he got the best deal for himself. As I have already noted, commercialisation is part of the problem with modern-day football. We must not forget that Cruyff was the first real 'superstar', the first commercial player. However, even when creating his brand, he drove the game forward.

It was almost thanks to him, fresh from his teenage years, that Ajax became a professional football club. At times, his personality, ego and ruthlessness did hurt people's feelings, even those close to him, but his goal was always to push the boundaries and achieve what he cared about so dearly – not just football, but entertaining football.

We should be thankful for the mass exodus of sailors, bankers, entrepreneurs, teachers and British citizens from all walks of life in the late 19th century whose journeys seeded football into different cultures all over the world. It is worth noting that the British football associations played their part.

Football was not something they wanted to keep a secret; they employed players and coaches to help spread the joy of football to the rest of the world. For this story, however, we must begin with the tale of what John Tait Robertson and Jimmy Hogan created in Budapest, something that, when you join all the dots, can almost certainly be classed as the base of what would make up the nucleus of *Totalvoetbal*.

Part One

The Hungarian Roots

AS JONATHAN Wilson states in his book *The Names Heard Long Ago*: 'Hungary taught the world to play; we're all the protégés of Jimmy Hogan now.'[3] So, with that in mind, the story of Hogan and what happened in Hungary must be told. Although he may not have a direct link to the birth of Total Football, you can't help thinking that, without these early developments in the game involving him, there simply wouldn't be Total Football. A point I want to reiterate is that, although I am telling the tales of certain teams and coaches, I do not want to label any of them as the founders of Total Football until the parts focusing on Ajax and the Netherlands. Ultimately, Total Football was born and created in the Netherlands, but the journey this book will take us on will hopefully not only shed some light on what inspired Total Football to be created but will also help distinguish what attracts us, as fans, towards it.

Jimmy Hogan, without doubt one of the most influential pioneers of the early game, helped spread it across the continent with revolutionary ideas. He is often cited as the man whose work helped create the great Hungarian team that would go on to humiliate England 6-3 on 25 November 1953, but I want to look at the work of the Scotsman, John Tait Robertson, and what he brought to Budapest in 1911 before Hogan arrived in Hungary, I am going to argue that it was Robertson who created the pathway for the great Hungarian side, a theory supported by Ashley Hyne in his book on the career of Jimmy Hogan. The fact the base came from a Scotsman is integral when looking at the state of football in the late 1800s.

The Scottish combination

The English upper class created football to be a dribbling game and, to their disgust, they couldn't quite fathom the Scottish combination game, as it came to be known. Right from the inaugural international match in 1872, in which Scotland held England to a 0-0 draw, the Scots outplayed their neighbours. Scotland faced clear disadvantages; not only were they a physically smaller team, they only had players from Queen's Park to choose from and were inexperienced compared to their English opponents. This forced them to look at new ideas. The Scots decided they would move away from the charging game favoured by the English and invented a 'pattern weaving' approach. Scotland started with a 2-2-6 formation against England's 1-2-7 and the aim of the game was to keep the ball away from the English. The focus on passing was unique at the time; it is often said that, before this game, the English never passed at all. Glasgow-based Queen's Park, Scotland's first serious club, made the Scottish style famous.

Initially, the play was quite slow and not particularly effective and only really included one aspect of what would make up the general basis of the combination game: passing. Early on, it was successful enough against the rigid individuality of the English. In the first 16 official internationals against England, Scotland won ten and lost only twice and the English were forced to move away from their dribbling and charging. The passing masters were certainly Queen's Park and their side contained some of football's greatest pioneers.

Clubs everywhere started to adopt the passing style. Queen's Park eventually fell asleep on their throne, allowing clubs all over the isle to adapt and progress their style. However, it wasnot a level playing field. Scottish clubs, hindered by their strict amateur status, saw English clubs lure away their talented players. The main focus in England became winning, whereas playing the game in the right or best way had been the objective in the early years. This characteristic of playing football in the right way is shared today by admirers of Total Football. Never mind the tactical implications the Scottish were introducing; just as important was the culture they instilled in the game. The pride of how you played it. Yes, this culture began with a tactical idea – how to counter English supremacy – but, along with the success, it also helped unearth a better sense of what the game of football was and would be.

Even at this early stage in the game, it was not just the English who were looking to learn from those footballers who preached the Scottish style. Formed in Glasgow in 1887, Celtic were invited to tour central Europe in 1904. John Madden played inside-right for Celtic on that tour and, subsequently, was offered a coaching role in Prague. He accepted and was the man who introduced the Scottish style to the continent.[4] As it relied on team cohesion, the Scottish style must have included a lot of training using a football. This was not common elsewhere. Bernard Joy was an amateur footballer in the 1930s who, although registered as a Casuals FC player for most of his career, had a spell with

Arsenal and, in 1936, became the last amateur to be capped by England. After the Second World War, Joy never returned to his professional job as a teacher. He ventured into football journalism and his book *Soccer Tactics* helped shed light on the Scottish game. He described an attacking, pattern weaving formation with 'the half-back, the inside-forward and the outside-forward working in unison by short passing to one another on the move … the wing-halves pressed upfield to provide the base of a triangular movement which carried the ball forward with dainty inter-passing. Final touch was usually left to the winger who did not attempt to cut in, but lobbed the ball into the middle from the neighbourhood of the corner flag.'[5] Although it was not necessarily tactically effective, what this style of short passes allowed was for teams not to be constantly caught offside. Before a change in the laws in 1924, it was easy to catch attacking players offside. The fact that Joy comments on the triangular movement is also important; the triangle base is still implemented now as the foundation of possession-based football.

The ground-breaking nature of Scottish football was not just tactical. Training concentrated on providing the players with a fundamental skill set that allowed them to be comfortable on the ball, controlling and passing it well. This allowed them to pass the ball crisply and confidently, enabling zig-zag passing sequences that would carve open teams from out wide.

Joy wrote: 'It was a bit staid and perhaps lacked imagination, but it was polished, correct and attractive to watch.' This mastery of the ball has become the foundation for many of the coaches captured in this book. As Johan Cruyff would later say: 'There is only one ball, so you need to have it.'

The English finally started to take notice of the Scots and many Scottish players and managers were employed by Football League clubs as, although by the early 20th century there was a general acceptance among the English of the effectiveness of the passing game, the Scottish were still seen as the masters. The Scottish influence is illustrated by the so-called 'world championship' game, held in Edinburgh in 1895, in which English champions Sunderland beat Scottish champions Heart of Midlothian 5-3. The fact that all 22 players on the Tynecastle Park pitch were Scottish proves where the talent lay.

The Scotsmen

At the back end of the 1800s, Robert Smyth McColl, perhaps the greatest centre-forward in Queen's Park's history, went on a fantastic goalscoring spree for his country, netting 13 goals in 13 games. In 1900, the run would reach its peak in a game against England at Celtic Park. In a 4-1 win, McColl scored a hat-trick in what would be his final international. McColl was tempted south of the border, to Newcastle United, by a £300 signing-on fee and the chance to become a professional. McColl used £100 of his signing-on fee to go into business with his brother Tom. The newsagent R.S. McColl, which still exists today, was set up by the McColl brothers thanks to Newcastle United signing 'Toffee Bob', the nickname Robert acquired after starting his business. Next time you're in your local McColl's, remember to acknowledge Robert's role in the history of football and, more significantly, Total Football, because McColl's time at Newcastle United, albeit only three years before he returned to Glasgow to sign for Rangers, was long enough for the seeds of the passing game to be sown into their play.

It was at Newcastle that McColl inspired left-half Peter McWilliam, another Scot. McWilliam was signed from Inverness, so was not quite as educated on the passing style as McColl, but he would learn. McWilliam was so entranced by McColl's ideas that, when he became a manager, he took those ideas everywhere he went. Most importantly for our story, it was during McWilliam's second spell at Tottenham Hotspur that he brought through three players with great significance to the development of football – Arthur Rowe, Bill Nicholson and Vic Buckingham. The latter is perhaps the most significant for the Total Football story and we will examine this in detail further down the line. Rowe's impact cannot be ignored either; he would meet with the great thinkers of Hungary and help lay the foundations of the great Hungarian team of the 1950s in a sort of domino effect, with the final piece clicking Total Football into activation. It was arguably Rowe's impact in mentoring Buckingham as a young player that would inspire him to go into management.

Returning to the influence of 'Toffee Bob', this was not just beneficial for the Geordies. When McColl headed back to Glasgow, he would inspire another team-mate who would sail the seas to spread the word on how football should be played; John Tait Robertson.

* * *

Another character I want to mention, who appears to have had an impact on McColl and Robertson, was a man called James 'Jimmy' Jackson. Born in 1875 in Lanarkshire, Scotland, his family emigrated to Australia when he was a young child before moving back when he was 18. During his time in Australia, Jackson played Australian Rules football. The game shares some similarities with association football but, tactically, especially in the late 1800s, it was a game based much more on freedom of thought among its players rather than the rigid, conservative style of association football in Britain. So, by the time Jackson made it back to home soil and started only kicking the ball and not picking it up, he already had a more creative palette. Starting out in the junior ranks of Scottish football, mostly playing as a left-back, he had a short spell with Rangers in 1896 before moving to Tyneside and signing for Newcastle United. But what is the link between an Aussie Rules player turned professional footballer and the concept of Total Football? Jackson played as a 'runner' in his Aussie Rules days. This position is effectively the player who, while offering support to defenders, also has to back up the attackers. So, at Newcastle United, the club's strong links to the Scots helped pair Jackson's Aussie creativity with the technical ability the Scots would have taught him. This was just before McColl signed, but there is no doubt that Jackson had left his mark on the Geordie crop he left behind when he signed for Woolwich (who later became Arsenal). He also left Newcastle in the First Division after helping them to promotion, allowing McColl to inspire the Geordies at the highest level in English football.

After sharpening his skills at Rangers and Newcastle, Jackson was now ready to impose his tactical ideas on his new team-mates at Woolwich Arsenal. Under the management of Harry Bradshaw, who appointed him captain, he was fresh from a promotion from the Second Division with Newcastle and now had it all to do again. With the team plodding along in the Second Division, they badly needed some inspiration. Jimmy provided it, his fresh ideas giving Arsenal a new dimension, most notably his 'double cover' idea. This was innovative, as well as successful. What

Jackson promoted was that when either full-back advanced forward, the other full-back would file across on the diagonal to provide cover for the space vacated, supporting the player pushing forward. This would kick-start a natural revolving motion of the whole team, causing the respective wing-half to fall back into a more defensive role with everyone else shifting position around the centre-half. This unlocks the link to Total Football. Players were now asked to perform roles that were the complete opposite to their starting line-up position. Forwards became defenders and defenders found themselves in attacking roles, both wide and through the middle. Jackson's genius didn't stop there. When the situation required, Jackson showed his versatility even more. He would often instruct centre-half Percy Sands to play as a 'third back', a role that shared many characteristics with that of the 'sweeper' many years later. You could argue that this was the first real sighting of that role. The third back did not so much start the attack, but he allowed the wing-halves to push forward and spring the attacks. This style would become known as the Whirl.

Again, if not a predecessor, the Whirl is certainly a distant relative of Total Football, something I will look at in more detail in the chapter on the Austrian 'Wunderteam'. It was a term used by Willy Meisl and referred to how football coaching needed to focus on allowing players to play with more freedom; something he credited to the style of play of his brother's Austrian team and which also sums up the style and beliefs of Jimmy Jackson.

Born in Dumbarton in 1877, John Tait Robertson, sometimes referred to as Jacky, was a half-back (essentially a midfielder in today's terms).[3] He started his senior career at Morgan in his homeland, before heading south of the border to Everton. He then won the Southern League in his only year at Southampton (1898/99) before his most dominant spell as a player after joining Rangers in 1899. In Robertson's first season in Glasgow, the club won every single league match. Robertson was a clever footballer and built up a fantastic bond with team-mates Nelly Gibson and Robert Neill. All three were specialists in the passing game to some extent, but Robertson was always pushing the envelope and striving for new ideas. It was Robertson who was the first footballer to use the pass back to his goalkeeper as a measure of protection from the pressing of the opposition. It is said to have been a vital tactic for Rangers in their invincible run of 18 wins in 18 games in a division which boasted many strong teams. When Robertson started passing the ball back to goalkeeper Matthew Dickie to reduce the risk of Rangers losing their winning streak, it changed the game.

Teams all over the world adopted this negative tactic, something that was only tackled with a rule change in 1992. William Wilton, the Rangers club secretary who doubled up as manager, allowed all the tactical decisions to be led by Gibson, Neill and Robertson. With the obvious base of the passing style, these three also boasted expertise in tackling and regaining possession. The tackling was not so much the art form displayed by the likes of Paolo Maldini decades later and Robertson was known for the odd bone-crunching challenge. He was also good in the air and, when added to his technical ability, he was a fantastic midfielder, even in today's terms.

McColl arrived at Rangers in 1904 and only spent a year or so with Robertson, but it was enough time to influence Robertson into being more proactive with the passing approach, something he would take to London and then Hungary. Robertson went on to win three successive Scottish titles but, more importantly in terms of his impact on the global game, was part of the Rangers team who toured Austria and Czechoslovakia in May 1904 in which the Scots won all six games comfortably (it is impossible to confirm, but it appears McColl was not on the tour). To help spread the joy of football to the world, successful teams would often be invited by their national association and entrepreneurs from the hosting countries to tour. Clubs would play exhibition matches, sometimes against teams from their own league who were also touring, with the hope of inspiring the locals into forming clubs.

After Rangers completed the 1904 tour, Robertson became the first player signed by Chelsea, who were London's newest professional club and boasted the capital's biggest football stadium … just no players to play in it. Gus Mears targeted Robertson as the perfect man, not only for his football ability but also to help find players for their inaugural season in English football (1905/06). Although only 28 years of age and I feel sure he would have had plenty of other offers, Robertson could not resist the call from Chelsea. He had the opportunity to not only carry on playing but to build a team from scratch for ambitious directors willing to open their cheque book. He had a mammoth task on his hands, building a club which had no players or supporters; he also had to play and win matches.

Thanks to the extensive list of clubs he had played for in England and Scotland, he had fantastic connections. He was able to call on friends and peers who had the correct skills and hunger to form a formidable side at Stamford Bridge. His name carried with it a sense of respect and old team-mates and former opponents were among those who answered his call and joined him in London. His first two 'star' signings were former opponents. William Foulke, nicknamed 'Fatty' thanks to his colossal 22st frame, was an England international. He was a football celebrity and it is said that attendances were boosted by several thousand every time he filled the goal (mainly out of sheer curiosity, I would think). Ireland's star winger Joe Kirwan was also recruited, with Robertson tempting him away from Tottenham Hotspur. I am sure money was a factor in these big names joining a brand new club who were starting out in the Second Division, but the prospect of playing for and with a charismatic footballing brain like John Tait Robertson must also have excited them.

However, the side Robertson was assembling was not some type of all-star team. He could not simply count on a cast of big-name players deserting the First Division to join him at Chelsea. He also networked his way around other clubs to see if there were any players they might be letting go. This worked a treat, as Robertson was able to clinch deals for a host of experienced professionals for reasonable sums. He also held trials for enthusiastic local players who would hopefully add some depth to his squad. The response to these trials was hilarious at times; speaking to the press later that season, Robertson revealed some of the applicants' stories. 'Among the many applications I received was one from a man who said he was a splendid centre-forward, but, if that position was not vacant, he could manipulate a turnstile.' One aspiring player claimed: 'You will be astonished to see me skip down the line like a deer.' Another said: 'I'm willing to be linesman, goal-keep or mind the coats.' Although many would-be players were rejected, Robertson had a squad ready for the club's inaugural league game against Stockport

County, although a 1 0 defeat brought them back down to earth. Robertson – already Chelsea's first manager, first player and first coach – became the club's first goalscorer, too, when he scored the only goal in their second game, a 1-0 win against Blackpool. John Tait Robertson was able to build an ultra-attacking side that went on to register 90 goals in 38 games in that first season, including a 5-1 demolition of Hull City in their first league game at Stamford Bridge.

* * *

During the early 1900s, a series of books titled *Book of Football* were published and, in the 1906 edition, Robertson wrote of his team's style of play: 'The forwards can play the three inside game or indulge in those long, swinging passes out to the wings that are more effective against some teams.' This shows Robertson was moving towards adapting the original version of the Scottish style, opting for the interchanging of passes to be focused more centrally rather than on the wings. The terminology used by Robertson is also intriguing; he talks about allowing his players to 'indulge' in different patterns of play. To indulge in anything, you have to be deep within your comfort zone; this is even more relatable to football, where confidence works in harmony with a player's performance. Players who are comfortable in their ability and with their position will always perform better, allowing confidence to grow. Robertson's Scottish-style focus on mastery of the ball through training would have allowed him to give his players more freedom on the pitch to make their own decisions having armed them with a range of tactics and ideas. The long ball out to the wings that Robertson mentions was prominent in the English game; the centre-half would often switch the ball out to the wing, no matter the state of the play. This diagonal ball – or 'swinging' as Robertson describes it – can still be seen in today's football. However, Robertson and his colleagues weren't too keen on focusing their play on this style, believing it slowed down the attack and was too predictable. Robertson shied away from using the wings unless forced to, opting for the 'three inside game' he refers to in *Book of Football*. While he still wanted to implement the zig-zag combination of passes more centrally, he also wanted his players, should the ball end up on the wing, to pass the ball back into the centre of the field as quickly as possible. This shows that his thoughts were still very structured and quite simple. Nonetheless, it allowed his teams to be direct and the speed of transfer from defence to attack was perhaps the first of its kind. There is no doubt about it; John Tait Robertson carved himself into football history as the first coach to move away from the old leisurely passing tradition of Queen's Park and other Scottish team [4].

To allow his teams to drive through the middle of the opposition, with devastating pace, Robertson also reinvented the role of the centre-half somewhat. George Key was the centre-half for Chelsea. Also taken from his essay in *Book of Football*, Robertson mentions the role of Key in his side. 'He acted as a sixth forward and then assist[ed] the defence and generally ma[de] himself exceedingly inconvenient to opponents.' Was this the early beginnings of the sweeper? What is certain is that Robertson believed the centre-half role was as much about attacking as defending. You can't get much more Total Football than that.

Despite this fantastic debut season and being mentioned among the country's top teams, Chelsea finished third and missed out on promotion. The following season's objective was pretty straightforward – promotion. On the pitch, they looked in fine fettle to achieve this, but upstairs in the boardroom, Robertson was becoming a problem. His professionalism was under scrutiny thanks to a substance that would ruin so many great talents – alcohol. His whereabouts weren't always known and this problem went unnoticed until a board meeting in November 1906. Robertson was a no-show at the meeting and, looking back at the season's stats, he only played in three of the opening 12 games. His commitment was correctly questioned by club secretary William Lewis, the man who would replace Robertson as manager. The missed meeting would be the final straw for the Chelsea board.

On 21 November, Chelsea received the resignation of Robertson as manager, with a request that he could be released from his playing contract on a free transfer. Both requests were accepted, with the condition he did not join another Second Division club. Just over a month later, Robertson signed for Glossop in the Second Division as player-manager, breaking the agreement he made with Chelsea. However, Glossop were propping up the table at the time and were certainly no threat to Chelsea. The Stamford Bridge club went on to clinch promotion that season and it is clear their success was a result of Robertson's work. It was a great shame he could not be part of the celebrations, as it was the team he built, playing a style he created. Robertson spent two years at Glossop but was never able to recreate what he did in the capital. Leaving the club in 1909, he ended up at Manchester United for a brief spell as reserve team coach. It was during this time that Robertson needed to start afresh with a new challenge and Budapest was certainly that.

As Ashley Hyne points out in his book on Jimmy Hogan[4], Robertson established himself as pretty much the first modern coach by allowing more imagination from his players, moving away from the stale 'gentlemanly leisure of the great Glaswegian tradition'[4] and opting for a quick, direct, attacking style of play. This focus on transferring from defence into attack at pace proved attractive to central European fans. Crowds who grew up following horse racing and wrestling demanded excitement and drama. [4] Robertson's motivation for this style of play was most likely purely down to his beliefs on how the game should be played and that it was the best way to get results. But even in 1910, before the Europeans had really got stuck into the game of football, they already demanded a certain style of play. There is a lot of literature on how England taught the world the game only to be left behind and plenty of books go on a journey to find the answers behind this. For me, the demands of the fans has to be one of the most important factors. League tables, pundits, stats; they all contribute as feedback for teams and coaches on how they are performing. But, ultimately, if the fans aren't happy, that is when something has to change. I have already mentioned how the journalism of the 1960s and 1970s influenced my father's views on the game, helping him become more conscious of what quality football was.

When Robertson arrived in Budapest, the demand for success was minimal. Instead, it was excitement and drama that brought in the fans. It was the fast-paced style that Robertson and others like him promoted; the hard-tackling, crisp-passing, fast football that attracted massive crowds during those 1905 tours in Vienna. In an era long before TV and sponsorship deals, the bigger the crowds, the more cash would be available to attract better players and improve the club's facilities.

Edward Shires was 17 when he abandoned his life and job at a typewriter factory in Manchester in 1894. His early work in sport was mostly based in Vienna, where he helped form one of the first football clubs in the city. A decent enough player, he also became the captain of the Austrian national team. In 1904, he moved to Budapest. He worked for the Underwood typewriter company[3] but he was also involved in importing sports equipment and promoting new ideas, most notably introducing table tennis to Austria and Hungary. Settling in a new community, he sought out a football team to play for. Shires joined MTK. Magyar Testgyakorlók Köre (the circle of Hungarian fitness) were a club who originally focused mainly on fencing and gymnastics before branching out into football in 1901. Their first ten years were rather dull and, although they won two titles, they were miles off the dominant side in Hungary, Ferencvaros.

Alfréd Brüll, a businessman, took over as president when MTK won their first title in 1904. Shires retired from playing after this triumph, taking on a more administrative role, as well as working as a referee.[3] The club won the title again in 1907/08 but the following years were dominated by Ferencvaros until Shires inspired some drastic changes. In 1911, he managed to negotiate the signings of two British imports. Joe Lane, who was an English centre-forward who signed as an amateur, scored the only goal in a win against Ferencvaros in the opening match at MTK's brand new stadium, the Hungaria Koruti Stadion. The other British import was, of course, John Tait Robertson.

Robertson was at Manchester United as assistant manager when Shires got in touch. Shires feared it would be difficult to persuade him to move to Budapest but, unbeknown to him, Robertson was on the hunt for a new challenge. Despite all he had done for sport in general across Austria and Hungary, Shires felt his proudest achievement was convincing Robertson to accept the role as MTK manager. 'It was Robertson who did the most for developing football in Hungary,' Shires said.

However, when Robertson arrived in Budapest, he wasn't impressed with what he found. He told a Hungarian newspaper: 'The mistake the players commit ... is that they only use one foot.' He also said: 'The aerial game is very weak ... the half line does not play well with the backs; when the backs lose the ball, the halves should be there to provide cover. The halves are not working together with the forward line either, and their shots are not good.' These comments show just how much work he had to do if he was going to implement his style of fast-paced football from defence into attack. But this is why Shires wanted him; he recognised this style would be attractive for the fans and bring success.

In many ways, Robertson's task at MTK was even harder than his job at Chelsea, where he had to start from scratch. Here, he had to change the mindset of the players and develop their attributes, but he succeeded in both. Although Ferencvaros won the title in 1911/12 and again in 1912/13, making it five in a row, Shires was happy with what he was seeing. 'Because of Robertson's work, and the example set by Lane, the MTK style was created and MTK became a stronger and stronger opponent for Ferencvaros to face.'

In the summer of 1913, history repeated itself. Robertson returned to Scotland and, in an interview in 1933, Shires said: 'It is a pity that he wasn't teetotal. If he had been, he could still be around now.' Just as at Chelsea, his love of alcohol must have played a big part in his departure and, again, he was not able to enjoy the success of the team he built.

MTK ended the dominance of Ferencvaros by winning the league title in 1913/14 under the management of Bob Holmes. He had played for the great invincible Preston North End team, who had strong Scottish roots embedded in their success. After Robertson left, MTK went through a number of managers and coaches before finally settling on Holmes. However, to illustrate the impact Robertson had on MTK, shortly before he arrived in 1911, MTK hosted a Blackburn Rovers team managed by Holmes and Blackburn won comfortably by 4-0; just after Robertson left in May 1913, Blackburn returned, this time as English champions, and were beaten 2-1. Under Holmes, MTK won the title, finishing the season unbeaten and smashing Ferencvaros 4-1 in the process.

Holmes's work was disrupted when, with the First World War taking a turn for the worse, he left in 1914. With the war also disrupting the league calendar, there were three shortened unofficial seasons played, MTK winning the last of these before the full league resumed in 1916/17. The club needed a new manager to help carry on the work of Robertson. As Shires put it: 'The Hungarians learned more from him in two years than they would have learned from somebody else in ten.' What grew from this period in Hungary was a monster; not only did the Hungarians go on to become one of the greatest national sides in the world, but the number of coaches and footballing brains who emerged in the 1920s and 1930s are arguably the most influential and important class of students ever to bless the beautiful game. More recently, the only two clubs who can claim to have generated so many coaches and future coaches are Ajax and Barcelona; and I feel Total Football is the spine of it all.

The birth of the football coach

In 1916, the powers in charge at MTK turned to another Englishman, one who was currently imprisoned in Vienna. Jimmy Hogan had been a decent professional player with Burnley, Nelson, Fulham, Swindon and Bolton. But it was always the thought behind the game that interested Hogan and he set his mind on coaching once his playing days were over. What motivated him to become one of the greatest-ever coaches? Well, in 1904, during his time at Burnley, upon blazing a shot way over the bar, he turned to manager Spen Whittaker, hoping for some coaching as to why he misplaced the shot. 'Just keep having a pop, lad,' Whittaker told him. 'If you get one in ten, you're doing well.' It is scary to think such comments are still heard today from coaches up and down the country. This was no good for Hogan; he wanted answers and, from then on, dedicated himself to understanding technique. For me, I remember the first time I heard players like Bergkamp or came across quotes from the likes of Cruyff and Van Gaal on technique and how important it was. It was a revelation to me. My own experience in football was littered with army-type instructions from coaches. 'Run faster, tackle harder, put your laces through it.'

With the Scots already focusing on technique, mainly in terms of passing, the foundations laid by Robertson provided the perfect platform for Hogan to build on when he arrived in Budapest. Applying his great coaching ability and excellent training methods, he took MTK and football in Budapest to the next level. For Hogan, his relationship with referee and FA agent of sorts James Howcroft would prove to be his most vital friendship in relation to his coaching career abroad. Although Howcroft lived in Bolton, he had officiated many internationals – mainly featuring the Netherlands and

Belgium – and became very familiar with the hierarchy at the Dutch FA. During the 1909/10 season, Hogan was still in his playing days and having a terrible season with Bolton. This is said to be when he first had a conversation with Howcroft about coaching overseas.

The Dutch had already started to import British influence into their footballing culture in the early 1900s. It was actually a tour by the Robertson-inspired Chelsea side of 1907 that opened the eyes of the Dutch as to how good football could be. The following year, Everton joined Chelsea in the Netherlands and the Dutch were left with the firm conclusion that they needed British coaches. Finances were limited, so each time an appointment was made, extreme caution was exercised and the Dutch sought much consultation before making a decision. In 1909, Hogan's Bolton team toured the country and hammered Dordrecht 10-1. Referee Howcroft provided a perfect reference for Hogan to the Dutch FA and the opportunity to coach in the Netherlands arose. What is not certain is whether the move was instigated by Howcroft or Hogan. Bolton were going through a torrid season and money troubles, so was it a financial boost for Hogan? Or did he want the chance to travel abroad to help spread the game he loved? Hogan is often portrayed as a football-obsessed coach who did it all for the love of the game. This may be true, but he was certainly a character who always made sure he got the best deal for himself, just like the man who is the heartbeat of this book, Johan Cruyff. Some reports suggest Hogan decided to go abroad because he was disenchanted with the standards of coaching in Britain. However, it is clear the deal was beneficial to Bolton (who would now not have to pay his playing salary), to Howcroft (who would receive a scouting fee) and, of course, to Hogan (who was offered a two-year contract, something he would not have had as a player at Bolton). Whatever the motives, Hogan later wrote: 'I was young and foolish enough to go abroad.'[8]

So, in May 1910, Hogan set sail over the North Sea to the Netherlands to take up his job at Dordrecht. Hogan quickly concluded why the team were struggling so much. 'They were fond of the pleasures of life, such as smoking and drinking.' The players were not really motivated; they were financially comfortable and played the game only as a spare time activity. But Hogan noticed something that seems to be built into Dutch culture, especially Dutch footballing culture. Despite their wealth and laid-back personas, the Dordrecht group were educated, professional and wanted to learn how to play football – the polar opposite to the footballers Hogan had left behind in England. This is perhaps the first meaningful plot in the map of the Dutch footballer for our journey to Total Football. Often, this studious characteristic is associated with the youngsters of the Ajax academies and other footballing schools in Holland, but more than a century ago the Dutch were willing to listen and learn. In England at that time, training with a football did not exist and neither did coaching; training was more of a military-type exercise than a football coaching one. The Dutch introduced to Hogan what he wanted from players; footballers in Holland did not feel embarrassed or belittled to be told how to play and, even more specifically, how to kick a ball. The logic of using a ball in training made sense to the Dutch, something that could not be said of the British at the time. This is something that, to this day, some managers and coaches in England, especially from my experience in the game, regard as a treat.

For example, pre-season (although the narrative is finally switching) would often be based around never touching a ball. Is it any wonder why we produce teams who will run around all game but have poor technique? Hogan's early coaching sessions in the Netherlands saw him devise drills to improve the players' heading, shooting and passing. However, his experience at Dordrecht did highlight shortcomings in his coaching ability. He was lacking when it came to developing a playing style and making the team gel, as illustrated by the lacklustre campaign Dordrecht endured under him, finishing sixth in the league. At the end of the season, the club decided not to proceed with the second year of his contract. Hogan, with his tail between his legs, returned to Bolton in 1911. However, Howcroft would again prove to be a pivotal figure in Hogan's career. Howcroft's glowing reference to the Dutch had backfired following Hogan's failure at Dordrecht.

Yet, in May 1912, Howcroft was again boasting about his friend's talents, this time to the Austrian coach Hugo Meisl. At a game between Austria and Hungary, which ended in a 1-1 draw, Meisl approached Howcroft to seek his opinion on who would be the best fit to kick-start the Austrian national team for the upcoming Olympic Games. Howcroft recommended Hogan and, although Meisl must have known he was taking a slight risk in trusting his judgement, he accepted the recommendation and put in place an immediate contract with Hogan, allowing him six weeks to get the Austrian players ready for the Games in Stockholm, Sweden.

Meisl was born into a Jewish family in Bohemia, now known as part of the Czech Republic, and began his working life as a bank clerk in Vienna, having moved there as a young teenager. Despite the lack of interest in football, the young

Meisl could always be found kicking a ball about with his friends. His job in banking did not fulfil his life ambitions; instead, he used his job to get by and ensured he had enough spare time to focus on his real passion, football. Meisl not only played football (as a winger), he also dedicated his time to improving the reputation of the game. This involved not only working to enhance the quality of local teams and their facilities, but inviting foreign clubs to play in exhibition matches in Austria. He hoped the visiting teams would improve public perception and knowledge of football, helping them fall in love with the game that had won his own heart. This had an impact on what type of football was brought to the country. At this stage, it did not matter what Meisl considered to be good football; what he needed was big crowds. On a practical level, paying customers helped cover the cost of hiring out stadiums and officials. But Meisl also needed as many people as possible to see the show if he were to promote and grow the game. Meisl did not stage the games to make a profit. There is no doubt his main objective was to make football a sustainable sport, primarily in Vienna but also with the hope it would spread across the whole country.

With this in mind, it was British football that won over the hearts of the Viennese; the fast-paced, hard-tackling style is what the punters loved, a far cry from the football the Austrian national team would play in their 'Wunderteam' years and even further removed from Total Football. However, Hugo's brother, Willy, who became a famous football journalist and would relay these first-hand tales to the United Kingdom, claims it was chiefly the previously mentioned Rangers team who toured in 1905 who inspired the Austrians. This is supported by Jonathan Wilson in

Inverting the Pyramid: 'Everything Meisl did tactically could be traced back to a nostalgic attempt to recreate the style of the Rangers tourists of 1905; he insisted on the pattern-weaving mode of passing, ignored the coming of the third back, and retained a sense that a centre-forward should be a physical totem.'[1]

Another team the Viennese were exposed to in 1905 were Newcastle United and playing in that team was Peter McWilliam, again giving us that link to the great Scottish players of that era. Willy Meisl reported how tour matches involving English sides inspired the Austrian crowds, none more so than the game between Everton and Tottenham on 7 May 1905. Willy claimed the crowd had doubled from the previous games to 10,000 and that the crowd had never seen such tackling in an exhibition match that was played like a cup final.[8] After this match, the game of football was now firmly planted into Austrian culture; fans wanted to see more and more of it. As facilities and teams increased across the country, so did the amount of matches being played, which not only drove down quality but also meant that games were played in front of sporadic audiences.

In October 1911, the Austrian league was formed, following the same rules as the English league. The primary focus of the league was to improve the quality of the matches by having fewer, but also to promote the progression of the national team. This plan would hit a stumbling block in 1912, after the previously mentioned draw against Hungary. A poor display by the Austrians led to the decision that Jimmy Hogan was needed.

So Hogan agreed to the six-week contract offered to him by Hugo Meisl and, in May 1912, he arrived in Vienna. It was a drastic culture shock for Hogan and his family. 'To leave … dark, gloomy, industrial Lancashire for gay Vienna was just like stepping into paradise.' As the season ended in Austria, Hogan was tasked with coaching across the city's football clubs and also spending time assessing the players who would represent Austria at the upcoming Olympics.

His coaching style hit an immediate buffer, as his students in Vienna were less obedient than the Dutch players he coached at Dordrecht. There, his players were willing to listen to and learn from anything their coach said and demonstrated. In Austria, the players were not impressed. What Hogan believed was coaching was totally different to what the Austrians wanted. Willy Meisl wrote: 'It was in Vienna that [Hogan] discovered how primitive British training methods were.'[8] To Hogan, coaching was about letting the players watch him perform exercises and for them to copy him; teaching rather than coaching. Coaching differs from teaching, I suppose, in that, as a coach, you must transfer skills to the players by both physical and verbal encouragement. The coach must then analyse the players as they carry out these skills to make sure their points are not only being understood but also carried out effectively. Being around football my whole life and being coached for nearly 25 years, I know when I come across a poor coach. They usually have similar traits, telling you how to do it their way without any reasoning or rationale beyond seeing themselves as a better player than those they are coaching. Perhaps this is a result of them having played at a higher standard than the level they are coaching at, a characteristic not to be mistaken as the approach Rinus Michels was known for; this will come later.

At the time Hogan was working in Austria, it was not only early in his own coaching career, it was early in the development of football coaching in general. I would like to think his approach was not ego-based and that it was more of an uneducated trial. While Hogan brought knowledge and experience, Hugo Meisl brought a more human touch to the partnership and, once Meisl got wind of Hogan's methods being criticized, he had to step in. Meisl was fantastic for Hogan; he let him take over all aspects of the coaching, left him to get on with it and sang his praises in public. But, after concerns had been raised, the pair sat down and decided they must study the world of coaching more intently. In Willy Meisl's *Soccer Revolution*, he explained that they 'worked out a more satisfactory scheme, probably the first modern training schedule in soccer'. The two now focused their attention towards coaching styles and exercises which would best fit their schedule. They achieved this by countless test runs of the exercises. This is the moment when Hogan became the coach now revered in football history books. He carried out endless self-testing to ensure he could carry out the exercises perfectly himself and he also discovered that his students learned much better when something was broken down into bite-size chunks.

At this stage, Hogan was far from being a tactician or strategist, but he had an ability to self-analyse his work and pick out which parts the players needed. His focus on ball mastery would now reach greater heights. This was the base for the Hogan 'list' which would become so famous in the world of football. Every player coached by Hogan would have been familiar with this list, which contained 11 ways to bring the ball under control. As Rory Smith sums up in his book *Mister*: 'This included with the inside or outside of the foot, the head, the chest, the thigh or on the turn.'[10] The list was the foundation of Hogan's philosophy as a coach and his sessions almost exclusively involved using a ball. As he stated himself: 'Ball training, ball training and more ball training, until our players are complete masters of the ball.'[10]

Once his players mastered ball control, Hogan would turn to the finer arts of the game; passing, crossing, shooting and dribbling. This would again involve simple exercises drilled into the players through easy-to-follow coaching. Hogan's methods on the training fields would have met with Johan Cruyff's approval. In one of many timeless quotes, most of which can be found on his website, Cruyff said: 'I see touching the ball once as the highest form of technique, but to be able to touch the ball perfectly once you need to have touched it 100,000 times in training.' [11]

Hogan's new and improved training methods were accompanied by the insight of Meisl; it would be him that built the bond with the players to ensure they were on board with what Hogan was teaching. Meisl was a lot more than just the relationship-builder between Hogan and his players; there is no doubt that he also brought an abundance of knowledge which Hogan was able to mould into his own coaching style. In those six weeks Hogan worked in Austria, Meisl was constantly feeding him with information about different patterns of play, games he had seen and players he had noticed while conducting his football tours. In the lead-up to the Olympics, Austria were to play several friendly matches. Hogan received great praise from reporters back in the UK, mainly thanks to a 3-0 win over a strong Tottenham Hotspur team in early June 1912. As Ashley Hyne points out in his book *Jimmy Hogan*,[4] this credit was somewhat misguided.

Only weeks before the triumph over Tottenham, Hogan's Austrian team lost heavily to Woolwich Arsenal, prompting drastic changes to the squad. The addition of five players from Deutscher FC Prag handed the Austrians some of the finest players in Prague, who had no experience of Hogan's training methods and were thrown straight into the side to face Tottenham. With the new players, Austria took the game to Spurs and found themselves 2-0 up against a side who had just drawn and then defeated the Hungarian Olympic side in the earlier stages of their tour. With half-time fast approaching, Tottenham were finally finding their feet in the game and Austria were somewhat saved by the whistle.

At half-time, Tottenham approached Hogan and the referee and suggested they make a quick turnaround and begin the second half immediately, which was commonplace in games during this period. Hogan knew that the tourists had the wind in their sails and declined their request, knowing that the break would likely cause the Tottenham players to lose the edge they had found towards the end of the half. The unsporting tactic paid off; Spurs lost their momentum and plodded through the second half, conceding a third goal to give Austria what looked like a fantastic win. 'If Hogan was trying to build a reputation for himself, it was an effective but shoddy way to do it,' Hyne wrote.[4] He is right, but the incident shows how far good results can obscure our vision of what is great football. Without this win and the boost it gave Hogan's reputation, he may never have been given the opportunities later in his career which paved the way for the emergence of some of the world's greatest teams.

* * *

The Olympics would, in fact, highlight that Hogan was still some distance away from being a top coach. The tournament ended in disappointing fashion for Austria and their play could not have been further from Total Football. Despite all the training sessions being focused on technique, the football played by the Austrians suggested they had been trained on how to kick the opposition, not the ball. Chasing success over philosophy? Perhaps, but also having only six weeks to prepare was certainly a challenge. They started off with a win over Germany, but it was a performance which revealed a lack of composure, with some good combination play let down by poor finishing. A second-round tie against the Netherlands seemed like the perfect game for Hogan to show some of his old pals just how far he had come after his spell at Dordrecht. It would be a performance that would never leave Hogan's thoughts – and not for the right reasons. The Dutch were far more advanced in both tactics and quality. Edgar Chadwick, a member of the Preston North End 'Invincibles' of 1888, was the manager of the Dutch side who dismantled Hogan's Austria.

The Netherlands were 2-0 up after only 12 minutes and the Austrians looked totally lost. Although the game ended 4-3 to the Netherlands, the winning margin should have been far wider. Almost 40 years later, Hogan would claim in his column for *Sport* magazine that the Dutch victory was not down to the management of Chadwick but, in fact, his own work in the Netherlands. Chadwick managed the Netherlands for five years, including two Olympic Games, before going on to manage Sparta Rotterdam, where he won the 1915 Dutch title. Yet Hogan wrote of the Netherlands' victory over Austria: 'They had the benefit of my coaching in the years before I started my work in Austria.'[4] This was another Hogan trait; he played the media very well throughout his career. The *Sport* readership would not have known about Dordrecht's results and performances under

Hogan. Despite their defeat by the Netherlands, Austria's Olympic campaign was not over yet. They were consigned to the consolation tournament, in which they reached the final, setting up a meeting with Hungary. This game was a mess, more like a royal rumble seen in a wrestling ring than a football match. Hungary ran away with the match in the end but, more significantly than the result, the game highlighted problems with both countries' playing capabilities.

Hogan returned to Bolton for one last season as a player, a season in which he rarely featured, and he found himself looking for a job abroad again in the summer of 1914. He was offered the Germany job, with the task of success at the 1916 Olympics their main objective. This would give Hogan nearly two years to prepare compared to the six weeks he had with Austria. However, when Hugo Meisl heard about the offer – he was asked by the German FA to supply a reference – he contacted Hogan to offer him another job in Austria and snatched him away from the Germans. Although 1914 would see the outbreak of the First World War, no one knew what was around the corner at the time Hogan accepted the job, with Winston Churchill declaring that Europe was a region of 'exceptional tranquillity'.

So, off the Hogan family were again, back to the familiar territory of Vienna. Hogan returned to Austria full of confidence, armed with a better understanding of the Viennese people and, more specifically, the players he would be coaching. Meisl had set Hogan a mission to visit the top clubs in Vienna. FK Amateure Vienna and First Vienna Football were two of these and their teams included many of the players Hogan had coached at the Olympics. After Hogan's work was done on the training pitches, Meisl would invite him and his wife, Evelyn, for a lavish meal followed by enjoying a performance by the city's finest orchestra. The culture and way of life could not have been further removed from that being experienced by his counterparts in England who would have been coaching part-time alongside a gruelling low-paid job, then spending their free time sinking pints in the local boozer, surrounded by tobacco smoke and depressing weather outdoors. Hogan realised how fortunate his circumstances were and it influenced his coaching. Hogan once said: 'I have often compared Austrian football with the Viennese waltz, in that it is so light and easy.'[4]

In the streets of Vienna, which were beautiful and calm, locals would greet new faces with warmth and politeness; this mood helped Hogan come to the conclusion he could no longer ask his players to play the competitive, confrontational football he had been involved in throughout his career. It just wasn't in the DNA of the Viennese people, so why move them out of their comfort zone on a football pitch? They were proud enough of their characteristics to want to play football in a manner that best represented them as people, to create their own path, very much like the Dutch with Total Football. Is this why Total Football is always shot down within English footballing circles? Even as early as 1914, Hogan knew that changing the British mentality was a near impossible task. Although the British were always hailed as naturals of the game, they never wanted to learn, even in these early stages of football's evolution.

Players in the rest of Europe, however, were not only willing to listen to instructions, they were reflecting on them, analysing and adapting them to help make them better footballers. Hogan, now with a better understanding of his players, adapted the training schedule he first developed with Hugo Meisl in 1912. It now consisted of 'continuous ball practice, followed by side games. In the latter, positional play, movements, covering-up [marking], tactics and everything appertaining to the game, was drilled into my pupils.' [8] It is astonishing to think that Hogan's training regime in 1914 was similar to what coaches in England have only recently started to implement. Before 2010 and Spain's conquering of world football, the English opted for the same style Hogan disregarded back in 1930 as being out of date. Hogan wrote then: 'British training methods are out of date. As schoolboys, we learnt how to play the game by kicking the ball every day for hours upon hours and it seems strange to me that, when we become first league players, the ball work is dropped like hot bricks and we are trained for the game on running tracks or the golf links.'[10] That is nearly 100 years for the FA to change their syllabus and direction and still it doesn't feel natural to our country; perhaps it just isn't in our DNA?

* * *

The impact Hogan had on his Viennese students is debatable due to the short time he actually had to coach there. His first spell was only a six-week training camp for the Olympics and this time he wouldn't last much longer. Despite Churchill's claims of tranquillity in Europe, the scene dramatically changed after the assassination of Archduke Franz Ferdinand in Sarajevo. By early August, Hogan didn't really know where he stood amid growing concerns over the state of Europe and he approached the British embassy looking for answers. He would later claim he was reassured there was no immediate danger and that he should carry on working as normal. Within 48 hours, war was declared. On 4 August 1914, Hogan, a British citizen in a hostile city, found his home being raided in the early hours of the morning and he and his family were arrested and imprisoned. Later, his wife and children were released and placed under house arrest. Hogan, however, remained a prisoner. The two-year contract he had signed with the Austrian FA had been terminated, leaving his family in a tricky situation. Finding themselves in a foreign country with little money, they struggled until finally being granted permission to return to England in March 1915.

The treatment of his family enraged Hogan, perhaps even more than the state he found himself in. Hogan would, eventually, also be released from prison and was placed under house arrest thanks to a generous intervention by a wealthy expat family. The Blythes had lived in Vienna since the 1870s and made their fortune selling clothes. They were also good friends of Edward Shires. Hogan would no doubt have remained a prisoner for the remaining years of the war had it not been for this intervention. Instead, he spent the war years teaching the Blythes' children English and various sports. Despite this relatively pleasant environment, Hogan would go after the Austrian FA in 1919 when he finally got back to England. He wrote an open letter claiming the Austrian FA had broken his contract and left his family to starve. He called on FA secretary Sir Frederick Wall to sever all ties with the Austrian FA.

Hogan's spell at the Blythe family home would come to an end thanks to a call from Budapest and MTK. I touched on his appointment at MTK earlier in the book but, now we have a background on Hogan himself, I want to focus on the new environment he would be working in.

Hogan described Budapest as the most beautiful city in Europe. Despite the war, Budapest was very much still a functioning, busy, modern capital. Edward Shires claimed

Hogan had written to him from his captivity in Vienna asking for help. Shires turned to his friend, businessman Alfréd Brüll, once again. Brüll was described as 'one of the biggest-hearted men living'.[3] It is also thought that he had made it his mission to help out any Englishman who found himself in trouble but, as Jonathan Wilson describes in *The Names Heard Long Ago*, he must also have appreciated the opportunity to bring in such a well-skilled coach to propel MTK's success to the next level. Whatever the motives behind hiring Hogan, he arrived in Budapest in late 1916. Bob Holmes had left his post as manager after the events in Sarajevo, not waiting around to see how things panned out. He headed over the Irish Sea to manage Cliftonville.

The war for Brüll changed nothing in terms of his plans for MTK; he kept funding the club, constantly injecting funds from his own pocket. Meisl wrote in *Soccer Revolution* how Brüll allowed the club to go as far as it wanted, financing the development of a brand new stadium in 1911. This new stadium would be Hogan's new 'prison', an arrangement that suited both parties. MTK were without a coach since Holmes abandoned them two years earlier and there was no way Hogan could leave, as he was still under house arrest. It was, however, a very loose form of house arrest and it is believed he did get to venture around the city. Just as Hogan discovered the culture in Vienna had a huge impact on the players, he would find the same in Budapest.

The culture of Budapest

Coffee houses were the heartbeat of Budapest's culture in the early 1900s; it is estimated the city boasted around 500 at the time. In *The Names Heard Long Ago*, Jonathan Wilson assesses the importance of these coffee houses, not only in Budapest's society in general but in influencing the footballing culture. 'The coffee house was the symbol both of Budapest's modernity and of its Europeanness.'[3]

People from all walks of life gathered in them, from well-dressed entrepreneurs to working class people about to begin a gruelling day's graft, discoursing various subjects and interacting with one another on a daily basis. Wilson says: 'It was a democratic space in which different classes gathered to discuss the issues of the day; politics, art, music, literature, gossip and football.'[3] It was the freedom these coffee houses offered that was most intriguing, especially for writers, who would sit among the unsuspecting public and soak up the atmosphere. The stories told in these coffee houses were often published in local newspapers and magazines. Wilson uses a quote from a journalist named Sándor Bródy, who once wrote: 'To be in intimate contact with thousands of people, with every group and class, who discuss their most intimate affairs in front of one's eyes, this constitutes the very definition of heaven for the writer.'[3] The coffee houses were a hub for gambling on cards, dominos and other games and also offered an opportunity for more illicit behaviour, such as prostitution.

With all this in mind, imagine the atmosphere of these coffee houses and compare it to the pubs and bars in Britain as somewhere one might discuss football. As we stand up at an overcrowded bar, we are interrupted continuously by someone who has had too much to drink. They tell us how they would manage the elite football club you are discussing, offering random and unrealistic points of view, based on zero experience within the game – just a season ticket and 20 pints of lager swirling in their gut. Now, this can be fantastic entertainment, as you get to air your frustrations (especially as an NUFC fan) and take in some comical one-liners from pissed-up punters. But, in the Budapest coffee houses in the early 1900s, customers would be sat down at a table, where they would 'illustrate tactical arguments using the simple props of a cup, a spoon or a sugar bowl'.[3] Wilson points out that, once people were doing this in the coffee houses, it was only a matter of time before football professionals would begin to draw up diagrams and advance tactical discussions to a whole new level. Compare this to events in Britain. In the 1920s – two decades after these Budapest coffee house discussions were pushing the game forward – it was regarded as 'outrageous eccentricity' when the great Herbert Chapman began to introduce tactical discussions with his Huddersfield Town team.[3]

The level of ignorance within British football has been highlighted on countless occasions but what was perhaps most significant about the coffee houses was the backgrounds of those discussing the game. Football in Britain was started in the universities but, by the time it reached a professional level in the 1880s, football was in the grasp of the working class. When comparing those who attended games across Europe at the same time – and, more specifically, those in and around Budapest and along the Danube – there was a big difference, a real mixture of characters and, despite the game being dominated by men, women could be seen among the crowds, donning expensive clothing and extravagant hats. 'Ticket prices were so high that, for the majority of people, going to a match was a treat.'[3]

In terms of footballing knowledge and understanding, there would not have been much difference between British and Hungarian fans but I agree with Wilson when he states: 'They [Hungarians] expressed it differently, in diagrams and abstract thought.' [3]

Over a 40-year period, the British had already settled into a routine of playing in a conservative and restricted way. In comparison, Danubian football was a free spirit and the coffee house discussions blossomed into a football theory revolution. There is no doubt that the coffee houses had an even greater impact on Austrian football and this will be discussed in detail soon. In Hungary, there was another factor in Hungarian society which would impact their footballing identity. During the 1900s, as Budapest expanded, wasteland areas, lots or lumber yards would be left vacant. These areas were known as 'grunds' and would become playgrounds for local children. Ferenc Molnár's 1906 novel *A Pál Utcai Fiúk'* (The Paul Street Boys) tells the story of a group of children who, while enjoying their grund, encounter another gang who want to make it their own stomping ground. Much of the story is dramatised, but it sets the scene and culture of these grunds, some of which became famous around the city of Budapest for the standard of football being played on them by local youngsters. Indeed, Jimmy Hogan spotted two youngsters playing at their grund in the Városliget area in the city centre and György Orth and József Braun would be the final pieces in the creation of Hogan's fantastic MTK squad.

The grunds were seen as the perfect environment for youngsters to develop technique in much the same way that playing on the streets would help Johan Cruyff and Dennis Bergkamp hone their skills. The grunds had sandy, uneven ground with grassy patches throughout.[3] The ball, often made from cloth, couldn't bounce on this surface, meaning the kids had to learn techniques that allowed them to guide it, dribble and shoot in a way that it would stay off the surface, otherwise it would just get stuck. While the coffee houses were the base for the 'Danubian School', the grunds were certainly part of the base for the footballing culture that was to come in Hungary, but also in Argentina. In Ferenc Török's biography of Gyula Mándi, the Hungarian full-back and MTK player, he describes how the grunds were also important from a tactical sense. 'Since the occasional teams only had a goalkeeper as an emergency player, almost everybody had to defend and attack, too. This also meant that nobody on the square could act like a star. If anybody put on an act, the others either excluded him or taught him a lesson pretty soon.'[12] As Jonathan Wilson highlights, the importance of these grunds and the *potreros*, as they were called in Argentina, was similar and simultaneous in the two countries. However, as we will discuss later, the Argentinian footballing ideal was born out of an opposition to those who taught the game, the British, whereas the Hungarians 'happily followed where an enlightened British coach led'.[3]

MTK and Jimmy Hogan

Jimmy Hogan's house arrest allowed him to form a strong relationship with his MTK squad. With the manager based at the stadium, it allowed him to always be available should a player have any spare time or want extra training. Hogan, who was far from fluent in Hungarian, created a bond with his players mainly through the language of football. As he had discovered on his earlier travels, the young European footballers were thirsty to learn. The circumstances in Budapest also created an environment in which Hogan was able to forge bonds with those players who had bigger egos and, as Brüll was building an all-star team, this would be essential to MTK's success. Ashley Hyne describes the MTK squad Hogan had as 'the most talented side Hogan was ever to coach'.[4] The squad included three of the greatest ever Hungarian footballers – Kálmán Konrád, Alfréd Schaffer and Imre Schlosser. These three were already established stars in Budapest, but Hogan would add two youngsters to the roster who would perhaps exceed even the achievements of the established stars once they settled into this fantastic MTK squad. They were György Orth and József Braun, the two youngsters Hogan had spotted playing in the grunds. Hogan later said of the pair: 'They are mine, my very own.' This wasn't entirely true; they had both made enough ripples to be mentioned in football conversations in the coffee houses and were well known by clubs who played within the grunds.

Hogan, though, identified their hunger to learn and he wanted to teach, which would be an essential part of the footballing culture rapidly growing in Budapest. In an environment in which players were desperate to learn, they also did not have to battle opposition against self-improvement, something that, even as early as 1915, was beginning to hold back the development of the English game and its players. It would be the planting of a seed that would grow into one of the greatest national football teams of all time. Hogan's MTK side would win the national league five years on the trot from 1916/17 to 1920/21. Remarkably, MTK went undefeated in 1917/18 and only dropped one point; they won 21 games and drew the other, scoring 147 goals and conceding just ten. There is no doubt that the foundations of MTK's playing style had been laid by John Tait Robertson, illustrated in the way MTK passed their way to goal.

The team were also blessed with great individuals. In particular, MTK boasted a formidable front line featuring the skilful Konrad, prolific goalscorers Schlosser and Schaffer and the brilliant Vilmos Kertész. With Orth and

Braun acting as the suppliers for this forward line, it was no surprise that the squad went on to set such great records.

However, much of MTK's success must also be credited to Hogan and his ability to nurture and develop such rich talent. This team of all-stars included some big egos. Schaffer, a thunderous striker of the ball who was nicknamed 'the Football King', was well aware of his talents and would often strut around town as if he were a real king. The talented youngster Orth was also well known for indulging in self-congratulation. The biggest household name was Schlosser, who transferred to MTK from bitter rivals Ferencváros in 1916, having already won the league five times, top-scoring in each of those seasons. It would be Hogan's personable approach that proved to be his greatest asset at MTK. Yes, he inherited a fantastic squad, but it was coupling his friendly demeanour with his knowledge and coaching which allowed the players to achieve great success on the pitch. Players who played under him went on to spread their high-quality football throughout Europe, especially to neighbouring Austria. At MTK, the approach Hogan took to his work was similar to that in Vienna – total mastery of the ball. Robertson had drilled the passing game into the club's DNA and Hogan's obsession with working on technique and mastery of the ball enabled this team of stars to achieve the success their talent deserved.

The team only became so comfortable with receiving the ball, passing and moving thanks to the constant practice Hogan demanded. This meant that, even when he shifted players from one position to another, like when he switched Orth from full-back to inside-forward, it came naturally to them. Even before the ball arrived at their feet, the players knew where the next pass should be made. To play great football, there is no doubt you need great players. Many top managers have stressed this. Pep Guardiola often reiterates this point in press conferences when he is praised for his coaching methods and his successes.

Hogan was perhaps not as quick to hand the plaudits to his players and often received personal praise with a wide smile, but one cannot question his influence within the game and how he helped a certain brand of football to develop. After Hungary smashed England 6-3 in 1953, the head of Hungarian football Sándor Barcs was asked how Hungarian football had become so good. He replied: 'You had better go back 30 years to the time your Jimmy Hogan came to teach us how to play.'

In football terms, Hogan had perhaps the greatest job in the world. Yet, in January 1919, at the age of 36 and supposedly sick of football, he headed home, leaving behind his star-studded team. He was now unemployed and, with a wife and three children to provide for, he needed work. Not only did Hogan remain convinced the Austrian FA owed him money for what he believed was a breach of contract, he also felt he was entitled to a payment from the FA through its fund for professionals who had suffered financially because of the war. The story goes that Hogan applied to the FA for a grant, only to be shunned because he did not actually serve his country and, rather than receiving a cash payment, he was handed four pairs of khaki socks and sent on his way.

If this did happen, it would explain why Hogan, the former manager of one of the greatest club sides in European football, did not look for work in his homeland. It is impossible to know whether this humiliating episode actually took place, particularly given that Hogan, a man known for holding grudges, would go on to strike up a good relationship with FA secretary Sir Frederick Wall, the man who supposedly snubbed his plea for cash. The real reason Hogan never found work back in England was more subtle; the people in charge of the big clubs in England still believed there was no place in football for coaching and they certainly would not have paid anyone to provide it, regardless of their reputation. Hogan instead found work with the Walker's Tobacco Company.

As Ashley Hyne points out in his book on Hogan, his place of employment was situated in the heart of Liverpool's footballing world. Scotland Road was within walking distance of both the city's major clubs, Everton and Liverpool, but Hogan never once in the three years he worked there even bothered looking down the road for work at either club.[4] He knew his coaching work, so valuable to the Hungarians, was regarded as pointless in England. In 1922, Hogan left England again and took a job in Switzerland with Young Boys.

When Hogan left MTK in 1919, they turned to a former legend of the club, Dori Kürschner, to take the reins. MTK defended their title successfully, winning 18 games out of 22 and scoring 116 goals, showing that even without first Robertson and now Hogan MTK could carry on playing the way that brought them their earlier successes. At the end of the campaign, MTK went on a summer tour of Austria and Germany. With tensions growing in Hungary, and especially in Budapest, this tour would prove to be a welcome distraction for everyone involved. As the team moved through Austria, many of the travelling MTK players hunted for new clubs. Kálmán Konrád and his brother, Jenő, were signed by Hugo Meisl, who was now managing Wiener Amateure. Despite losing a number of players, MTK showed their dominance throughout. It was not just the acquisition of their players that impacted the clubs MTK faced, it was also their style of play. When MTK travelled to Germany and hammered Bayern Munich 7-1, local newspapers raved about their performance.

One report said: 'The visitors have developed a wonderful technique. Their playing ability is exemplary in every way. They are unmistakably fast in both their running and their treatment of the ball.' As a result of this game, the powers that be at Bayern decided they must adopt the MTK playing style. It was said that 'the class of the Hungarians is dazzling … [it's like] the Scottish game with all its finesse and precise ball handling'.[3] MTK lost another two integral members of their squad in Germany; Schaffer signed for Nürnburg and manager Kürschner joined Stuttgarter Kickers. Who could blame them for leaving? Not only were they able to obtain greater salaries, but also a guarantee of a safer lifestyle than that back in Budapest.

The start of the 'Danubian School'

Despite a depleted squad, MTK continued to flourish, mainly thanks to the playing style built into their DNA and the fact their recent history of success attracted players to sign for them. Two names that are of great significance to our story of Total Football would join MTK during this period. One was a 20-year-old full-back named Gyula Mándi, who was transferred from rivals Ferencváros after struggling to break into their first team. Mándi would become a stalwart for 18 years thanks to his great positional awareness and passing ability. Even more importantly, Mándi would go on to become an intelligent and influential coach.

MTK also signed the forward/winger Zoltán Opata. Mándi

and Opata would be hugely important in the great Hungarian side of the 1950s, as they were the real coaches behind the style of play, even though Gusztáv Sebes was the manager and received a lot of the plaudits. In the period from 1919 to 1924, MTK went through a number of coaches, mainly due to being unable to match the wages other clubs could offer and the unsettled political climate in Hungary.

However, the culture of the club allowed them to keep on winning, despite these turnarounds in management. Even without a coach, this brilliant MTK team functioned perfectly well. The players played almost by instinct, an instinct embedded into their style by Robertson and Hogan. From the 1919/20 season, MTK won six successive titles, extending their domination to nine a row since the league resumed after the war.

* * *

In 1925/26, city rivals Ferencváros finally broke MTK's stranglehold on the title, winning their first since 1913. This may have been thanks to the change in the offside law, which put a huge dent in the effectiveness of MTK's neat passing combinations. István Tóth, who was better known by his nickname 'Potya', was in his final season as a Ferencváros player when they reclaimed the title. Potya then became manager for the 1926/27 season, bringing revolutionary ideas to coincide with the new professionalism in Hungary. He was, in fact, Ferencváros's first professional coach. He would be the first Hungarian coach to introduce several important methodological innovations. These included warm-ups and different training techniques. Tóth, who shared similar traits to Hogan in terms of coaching style, was a great judge of talent and a fantastic motivator. Tóth was the first coach to establish a 'college of trainers [coaches]'. He put together the country's first coaching manual and stood at the centre of the key footballing figures in Hungary. Hogan, after his spell in Switzerland, did actually return to MTK in 1925 and, although the change in the offside law hampered them, the obsession with dominating possession kept MTK competitive and they put on some great shows.

However, the titles had dried up. Hungarian football would rise again, but, at the beginning of the 1930s, great Hungarian players and coaches were leaving the country and it would be Austria who were the first in line to feed on their knowledge as they started to spread their beliefs abroad. The 'Danubian School' had been born and six men, all players I have previously mentioned who went on to become managers, are integral to the story of Total Football – Kálmán Konrád, Alfréd Schaffer, Gyula Mándi, István Tóth-Potya, Zoltán Opata and Béla Guttmann.

Part Two

Along the Danube

THE PERFORMANCES of MTK and the football movement in Budapest were sending ripples right across Europe and nowhere would benefit more than Vienna from the Hungarian-inspired changes in football ideology. There were serious issues contributing to the development of football in Vienna. The threat of war in Hungary was a huge factor for Hungarian players and coaches who chose to leave for Austria, and money and general prospects looked much more appetising there.

The Hungarians would be bringing with them the wealth of knowledge and training techniques handed down by Robertson and Hogan. Also still in the picture was Hugo Meisl, who was waiting to mould these players and coaches, just as he did when hiring Jimmy Hogan ten years earlier. Meisl remained firmly intent on improving the Austrians' footballing ability. As with any great movement, the audience, participants or workers have to be on the same wavelength as those who are leading the drive.

The Viennese, with their passion for entertainment and class, provided the perfect canvas. The tours and exhibition matches organised by Meisl had got the Viennese taste buds flowing and, despite the poor results under Hogan, the national game was continuing to grow, partly thanks to his second stint in the city before he fled for safety in Budapest. In Hungary, it had been the discourse between fans in the coffee houses which inspired progress. In Vienna, café culture would take Austrian football to the next level.

Austrian football: the early days

The base of Austrian football had been developed in a non-professional environment with the forming of teams and clubs coming from cricket clubs and workplaces. British workers created clubs exclusively for the British citizens who found themselves in the city, which in turn created local sides to form and compete amongst each other. The year 1894 is credited as the birth year of football in Vienna. The First Vienna club was open to anyone good enough to pull on the shirt. Simultaneously, the Vienna Cricket and Football Club was formed, but only British players were allowed to join.

Between 1897 and 1900 there were 45 clubs based in the capital, which shows just how strong the game could and would become in the not too distant future.[13] In the years leading up to and during the First World War, participation in football in Vienna had developed and spread across much of the population. This, in turn, took the game away from just being played within sports clubs and in competitions. Football was now being played in the streets, parks and squares across the city.[13] A continuous theme in my mission to follow the road to Total Football is that it always seems to be developed from some sort of street or non-competitive free play; the grunds of Budapest, the street outside Johan Cruyff's house where he learned to play, the car park of Dennis Bergkamp's housing development where he developed his football technique or the Eyemouth beach my father always refers to as the greatest place to play football.

Football in Vienna was growing at a phenomenal pace; before the First World War, attendances would peak at about 10,000. By the time the game became professional, several stadiums had been built in Vienna and its suburbs to accommodate up to 80,000 spectators. Football was now just as popular as the cinema and towering over the social impact that music, art and literature were having on the Viennese public. In Britain, the game began in the public schools and middle classes but, by the 1930s, was very much a working class sport. In central Europe, this trend bounced in the other direction. When the bourgeois British brought the game across the sea, it was rapidly seized upon by the working classes.

As the game grew, the working classes were still represented in the form of the players, who would be playing the game at the highest level in central Europe, but the intellectuals had now found themselves entangled within the game. Their influence came mainly from the cafés rather than the pitch but they pushed the quality of football to another level. In Austria, football was very much a sport confined to the capital, as was the case with Budapest and Prague, a trend which saw these three capitals produce some of the best teams and players for almost three decades.

The coffee house, Scheiberspiel and the Viennese

At the centre of Austria's rise in terms of footballing calibre was the coffee house culture; more specifically, the coffee houses of Vienna. Each club in Vienna had its own café in which players, coaches, fans, officials and writers would mingle. The Ring Café became perhaps the most famous and was the central hub, as it was not confined to supporters of a certain club. It was also the place where Hugo Meisl would most frequently be found, lingering and plotting, discussing and informing.

These coffee houses did not only contain the footballing core of the city. Men and women from all social backgrounds gathered in them. With a bohemian and artistic feel to them, the cafés provided comfort for those who entered them. Despite the hectic activities taking place, from card games and chess to mail delivery and laundry collection, the cafés were a suitable venue for the intellectuals of the city to discourse on current affairs, art, literature and, of course, football.

The inclusion of footballers into the different cultures was starting to take hold. SK Rapid forward Josef Uridil was the first 'coffee house hero', as Jonathan Wilson highlighted in *Inverting the Pyramid*. His bullish playing style reflected his working class background and the fans instantly adored him. Those who were frequently in the Café Holub began to show an interest in him as his fame began to spread beyond football. He appeared as the main subject in a cabaret, advertised products ranging from soap to fruit, appeared at music halls and even starred in a film, playing the role of himself.

As early as 1922, business owners were starting to recognise the impact football could have on culture but, as important as football was becoming in Vienna, there remained an innocence around the game, with most Austrians regarding entertainment as more important than winning. To illustrate this, I have to discuss the concept of 'Scheiberspiel', which became famous in Vienna.

'Scheiberspiel' was a style born in the coffee houses which focused on technique and how the team must approach games with real tactical influence. The emphasis was on the team as a collective, rather than individuals being encouraged to win a game by themselves. The outcome of the match never really mattered. Win, lose or draw, the fans cared more about the art of the game they were watching than the result. In terms of playing philosophy, it was very much in the mould of the great MTK side from Budapest who had dominated in the 1920s. However, it is often noted that the Austrians had sped things up, with more complex combinations than the more traditiona play or Scottish Style.

Thanks to the upheaval in Hungary and the culture created in the Vienna coffee houses, football as a marketplace began to emerge in Austria. Since the best players in Austria were now being classed as stars, sharing and stealing the limelight from the actors, musicians, poets and writers, Austrian football began to invest heavily in bringing the best players to play in their country. At this time, the early 1920s, the best players were to be found in Hungary, just along the Danube River.

FK Austria Vienna and Hakoah were among the richest clubs in Austria at this time and managed to secure the signatures of Kálmán and Jenő Konrád, Béla Guttmann, Ernő Schwarz, Józef Eisenhoff and Alfréd Schaffer. The transformation of football into a professional game in Austria began to gain real traction after these signings. However, what is extraordinary is that this is also when 'Scheiberspiel' really started to dictate how Austrian football was played. These players came armed with the experience of playing in a style suited to 'Scheiberspiel' and, thanks to their quality, they helped promote a way of playing that helped it develop.

The Hungarian transfer market and Hugo Meisl's plotting

The main contributor in the development of 'Scheiberspiel' would be Kálmán Konrád's style of play. Hugo Meisl managed to bring him to FK Austria Vienna alongside his brother, Jenő, and Alfréd Schaffer. The three of them not only made the Austria Vienna side one of the greatest teams in the country as the club headed into the early stages of professionalism but also set a precedent for other players and clubs to follow. Their way of playing was quickly recognised as the right way to play the game, moving away from the kick and rush style Austrian football had previously been based on.

In Vienna, as the game headed towards the professional era in the years leading up to 1924, it was dominated by four clubs – FK Austria Vienna, First Vienna 1894, Sportklub Rapid and Admira. Up to 1938, when football returned to amateur status, these four clubs would help elevate the professional game in Austria to being one of the richest scenes in central Europe. SK Rapid and Admira were both formed in the suburbs of Vienna, showing that the game was now spreading not only throughout the classes but also outside the centre of the city.

FK Austria Vienna (also known as Wiener Amateur Sportverein or Amateure) were managed during this period by Hugo Meisl. His influence on football as a whole should never be underestimated – I have mentioned the work he did to bring the game across from the isles of the United Kingdom.

His constant desire to create a more competitive game led him to help create the International Cup, a tournament for national teams to compete in which was organised along the lines of the knockout stages of today's Champions League. This tournament would become the prequel to the modern World Cup finals. His influence on European club football and its competitions can still be seen on our football calendar. The Mitropa Cup was played in a similar format to the International Cup but was open to club teams, a prequel to the European Cup which, of course, later became the Champions League.

However, Meisl's input was so much more than just an administrative role. He coached not only FK Austria Vienna but also became the manager of the Austrian national team. During his tenure, Austria produced its greatest ever team, one that went so close to winning a World Cup and whose brand of football was remembered vividly by those who witnessed it.

They would become known as the 'Wunderteam' and fittingly represented the football played in Vienna, allowing the world to enjoy Viennese football just as much as the locals did when watching the city's club sides. Without the culture built around these clubs, the national team may not have ever reached the peak of world football. Without Kálmán Konrád, that culture would never have taken the path it did; he laid the foundations. His style, ability and beliefs were all instilled in him by John Tait Robertson and boosted further by Jimmy Hogan at MTK.

Kálmán Konrád was born in Bačka Palanka, a town beside the River Danube, before moving to Budapest as a young child. He joined MTK at the age of 14 and made his first-team debut at 17. I have already covered MTK's dominance in Hungary in the decade between 1910 and 1920, but to put into context how vital Konrád was to the team during the three seasons between 1917 and 1919,

MTK won 60 games, drew four and lost only two and he was an ever-present in the team, scoring 88 goals in this period alone. After the Great War, Hungary had become a Rightist country. The years leading up to 1920 were bloody and violent. They were fronted by Admiral Miklos Horthy, who came to power in 1920 after targeting communists and Jews with his politics and propaganda. Many Jews began to flee to neighbouring countries, so, when Hugo Meisl proposed the transfer to Konrád, football and money weren't his only motives; he was escaping what he believed was a broken country.

Again, John Tait Robertson can be credited with being the main contributor to the success of Konrad. It is believed that, when Robertson first arrived at MTK in 1911, he demanded to see a match straight away. After only 15 minutes, Robertson picked out one player and insisted he was going to make him into a star. That player was Kálmán Konrád and he would become the king of Viennese football.

Konrád brought with him a style that was already bedded into the Austria Vienna team, as they were, of course, coached by Jimmy Hogan between 1912 and 1914. But, although results improved for the club thanks to Hogan's coaching, it wasn't until the Hungarians were brought in that Austria Vienna won their first league title in 1923/24 and their first professional Austrian national championship in 1925/26. As clubs battled for key signings and more and more fans flocked to the stadiums, the Austrian footballing elite turned professional.

The first professional national championship was contested in 1924/25 and was won by a team whose success would also have a heavy Hungarian contribution.

The Jewish team that conquered the world

SC Hakoah Vienna, now almost forgotten, was a unique club. The football club was part of the Sport Club Hakoah founded by a group of Austrian Zionists in 1909 and built around the 'Muscular Judaism' phrase coined by Max Nordau in the late 1800s; he used it in an attempt to change the view promoted by anti-Semites that Jews were weak people. One of the first Jewish-only football clubs, Hakoah reached the Austrian top flight in 1920 just four seasons after joining the Second Division. In the years preceding the influx of Hungarians to the Austrian game, Hakoah had a number of links to the coaches who had helped influence football in Budapest. The team kicked on following promotion and, in 1921, hired a British man who had also played alongside Hogan at Bolton, William Brown (Billy) Hunter. The Scotsman followed a similar path to Hogan in terms of coaching. He worked for both Dordrecht and the Netherlands national team before the war.

Hunter forged quite a reputation in the Netherlands after ending up at Dordrecht a few years after Hogan and bringing the club success in the KNVB Cup in 1914. This is when he chose to take charge of the national team but, after only four games in the role, his career was interrupted by the outbreak of war. However, his impressive work ensured that his time in football was not over and he took charge of Hakoah in 1921. Hunter certainly seemed to be following the same ideas and methods as Hogan and, although Hogan is perhaps the more famous name, it could be argued that they influenced each other. Hunter was named joint manager of Hakoah with Arthur Baar, one of the club's founders, and together they helped produce football which won praise from the Austrian football critics and connoisseurs. Hunter was only involved for one full season but he helped steer the club to second place in the 1921/22 campaign. To ensure that they could compete with the best clubs in Austria, Hakoah began to invest money in hiring top coaches such as Arthur Gaskell, who also played alongside Jimmy Hogan at Bolton. It's hard to evaluate the impact that Gaskell had on Hakoah, as he only lasted a few months before departing; this is believed to be linked to the financial troubles the club had now found themselves in following promotion and it is important to remember that football in Austria was about to turn professional, which would have meant new financial commitments for clubs who wanted to challenge the big four clubs in Vienna. Despite the financial uncertainty, Hakoah managed to finish mid-table as Fritz Konus Kerr, who became player-manager, finished off the work of the British coaches. To stay within the group challenging for the title, it was imperative that Hakoah looked to improve the playing squad.

This is when they dipped into the Hungarian transfer market and signed goalkeeper Alexander Fabian (remarkably, he would go on to score a league title-winning goal after swapping positions with a team-mate after breaking his arm). He was joined by fellow countrymen Josef Eisenhoffer, Erno Schwarz and, the most important signing of them all, Béla Guttmann.

* * *

When Guttmann arrived at Hakoah in 1922, he was a well-known player along the Danube. He had made his international debut for Hungary in 1921 after joining MTK earlier that year. In that first international appearance, a 3-0 win over Germany, he was one of eight MTK players in the

Hungary line-up. His full-back partner was Gyula Mándi, another player who I will focus on as part of the 'Danubian School'. The role of the two full-backs at that time included being an integral part of beginning attacking moves. The position should not be confused with that of a modern full-back; the full-backs would line up in an area similar to that of a modern day centre-back. Before Guttmann joined MTK, Ferenc Nyúl had been a fixture at full-back and when he returned to Hungary after a short spell playing in Romania, Nyúl rejoined MTK and Guttmann was seen as dispensable. Guttmann was too proud to not be in the starting line-up and wass arguably too good not be playing regularly at the top level. So, in 1922, he decided to leave MTK and Budapest behind and head for Vienna. In *The Names Heard Long Ago*, Jonathan Wilson captures how even Guttmann's own wife questioned his motivation for joining the Jewish club Hakoah, stating that he didn't really have any ties to the Jewish faith or any religion.

Guttmann's move was probably motivated mainly by footballing and financial opportunities, but it also came at a time when many Hungarians, including footballers, were looking at ways to escape the right-wing and anti-Semitic culture evolving under the regent of the Kingdom of Hungary, Miklós Horthy. In the mid-1920s, a number of great Hungarian players began to migrate to Vienna. Many would choose to sign for FK Austria Vienna, as the religious background of Hakoah did not appeal to the players who were not Jewish, but Guttmann often claimed that football was not his main focus and that he was to be considered a businessman before a footballer.[3]

When Hakoah played away matches, they would be targeted by anti-Semitic abuse from the stands and even, at times, from opposition players. Fans saw playing Hakoah as 'playing the Jews'. The title-winning season was, as previously explained, settled in the most dramatic fashion but, over the course of the season, Hakoah had done more than enough to earn the title. They were pushed close by Hugo Meisl's FK Austria Vienna, with both teams playing the entertaining 'Scheiberspiel' way. Significantly, 1924/25 was the first professional season in Austria. Football was now a full-time occupation and Hakoah were the best team in the country, which was fitting considering Sport Club Hakoah, the sporting association that parented the football club, was one of the biggest sports clubs in the world. It boasted more than 5,000 members and offered a wide variety of sports. But domestic domination was not the only social purpose behind the club; they wanted to change anti-Semitic views, across the world, that Jews were unfit for sport. As a football team, they went on many tours of the continent in a bid to promote their competitiveness. A highlight of these early tours came in Britain when they beat West Ham 5-0 in 1923, the first defeat for an English club on home soil at the hands of a foreign team.

Although it took a number of years for the influx of new players from Hungary to help the club win the league in 1924/25, their influence cannot be underestimated, especially the work of Guttmann, both as a player and in influencing the playing style of the team. Hakoah played fantastic football on their way to winning the title but in the final weeks of the season, which was the first since Austrian football turned professional, the club again found themselves in money trouble. This unsettled financial position was always a threat to Hakoah's position at the top of Austrian football, but this mattered little to the club.

The Hakoah project was never about winning trophies; they existed to promote Zionism and raise money for the cause. But tensions were growing on the field as well and the season following their championship triumph proved to be too much, with Guttmann at the heart of it all. After beating West Ham in London, Hakoah had received widespread praise in the UK press and, at a time when British football was still revered on the continent, this was regarded as particularly significant.

Articles stated how the Hakoah side made great use of space and passed the ball beautifully. It was obvious that Hakoah's success was a result of being fully invested in the ideology of Hunter, Gaskell and, through the influence he had had on Hungarian players, Hogan. However, while the praise was clearly aimed at these coaches, Guttmann began to take some of the credit himself. He claimed that he was the most influential player against West Ham and that the win was the result of his tireless efforts to impress upon the team the philosophy and style he learnt at MTK thanks to his mentor Hogan.[3]

Guttmann would become quite a controversial character during his career; he was often outspoken and, in every country he found himself working in, was never far away from being called into the disciplinary offices of the football authorities. Guttmann explained in a newspaper interview that his decision to leave MTK for Hakoah was solely based on the fact he didn't have a stable source of income due to MTK's poor wages and that it had caused him heartache to leave the country and club he loved so much.[3] This sense of loyalty can be viewed with a pinch of salt. Across a 12-year playing career, Guttmann played for nine clubs, across central Europe and America. Despite becoming one of the most highly regarded Hungarian coaches of all time, loyalty and longevity are difficult to associate with Guttmann.

After the heights of the win in London in 1923 and the title win in 1925, results started to fall away, draws turning into defeats and wins into draws. Under the new offside rule, which seemed to favour a more physical approach, their short-passing combination game appeared to be less effective. Arthur Baar was still the top dog in terms of how the club moved forward and he decided to turn his back on the passing style. Guttmann claimed that his tireless work over a four-year period in establishing a successful style of play at Hakoah had been destroyed in a matter of months and that Baar had created an environment in which the other players no longer respected Guttmann.

Hakoah moved towards the snapping style, which was a much more direct approach and one which Guttmann believed the Hakoah squad were not built for, as they were all now masters of the ball thanks to their experience of playing the short-passing game. This trend still exists in football today; teams reach higher levels through new styles and ideas but, when they hit a rough patch, managers or directors pull the plug and revert to outdated tactics which, while they may steady the ship in the shorter term, take the club in the wrong direction. Although Guttmann displayed a lack of loyalty to the clubs he managed or played for, he was certainly loyal to the system he learned at his time in Budapest and MTK. However, just as John Tait Robertson is sometimes overlooked in terms of his contribution to the successes of Hungarian football, was the contribution of Hunter, Gaskell and the other coaches involved with Hakoah in the early 1920s overshadowed by the extrovert personality of Guttmann? Hogan and Guttmann both knew how to play the media in their favour but, when you delve deeper into the great teams of this era, it is often the more introverted characters, with little or no presence in the media, who appear to have been just as instrumental in creating success.

For Guttmann, it was his desire to travel and coach in different countries and continents which have given him such status in the history books of football and, when you add this to his clear dedication to the style of the passing game he inherited from his playing time in Budapest, he has to be recognised as one of the main influences on making this style a success around the world. He would go on to coach 25 teams across ten countries, as well as coaching several national teams. But, in terms of his impact on Austrian football as a player, his time at Hakoah was coming to an end. In 1926, Hakoah embarked on another successful tour, this time to the USA, culminating in a game at New York City's Polo Grounds in front of a record 46,000 spectators. Many of the Hakoah players welcomed the lack of anti-Semitism they encountered in the USA and decided to sign for American clubs. These players included Guttmann, who signed for a team in Brooklyn, New York. Several of the Hakoah squad who decided to stay in the USA ended up forming New York Hakoah, who would win the National Challenge Cup in 1929.

Hugo Meisl and his plot for international football

I guess that, by writing this book, I am seeking to bridge the gap between the football era I find myself in and one I was unable to experience; the era of Total Football and the days which shaped my father's love of football. Up to this point in the book, the name Hugo Meisl has featured on several occasions. However, it is now that I want to really focus on the man some call the father of modern football. In terms of bridging gaps, Meisl certainly built a bridge that allowed for the development of football across Europe. Not only in terms of organising the early football tours, hiring influential coaches and creating tournaments, but the fact he also created one of the greatest international teams in the history of the game. The Austrian 'Wunderteam' that took on the world in the 1930s would be the showpiece of all the work Meisl had done in terms developing football as a sport. This team brought pride to its country and provided a benchmark which teams and coaches still feed off to this day.

Meisl's tactical insight was inspired by the Scottish combination approach, backed up by his friend and colleague Jimmy Hogan. During the 1920s, Meisl focused on creating and sustaining professional football at club level in Austria. By the 1930s, the quality of the Austrian league was up there with the best in the world and this helped create a truly great national team. The 'Wunderteam' is perhaps the most referenced in terms of style and a sort of blueprint for the great teams that followed in the decades leading up to the birth of Total Football. The 'Wunderteam' are lauded as the first to use a withdrawn centre-forward – an early version of the 'false nine' – in the great Matthias Sindelar or 'Der Papierene' (the Paper Man). But this team also boasted the fantastic Josef Smistik, an attacking centre-half who mixed elegant crossfield passing with the breaking up of play. It was a team that relied heavily on patience and technique, backed up with a fluidity that spread throughout the 2-3-5 formation. All while staying true to the spirit of 'Scheiberspiel'.

This Austrian team has plenty of links to the Hungarian line-up of the 1950s and the Dutch side that produced Total Football. The most obvious to some is that, despite often being listed among the greatest international sides of all time, they never won a World Cup. This, for many, is enough to dismiss all three from the conversation regarding great teams. But what *is* success? Is it only judged across four weeks every four years at the World Cup? What these three sides created and displayed has lasted much longer than any World Cup win in the discourse amongst fans. The flow of Danubian football was flooding the thoughts of those who had witnessed it. There was a sense that this was now the way football should and would be played. So, in this sense, what the 'Wunderteam' did will never be erased from the history books. The 'Danubian Whirl' made fans and journalists understand a new dimension to football, setting a new baseline of what 'good' football was. They inspired coaches and players to spread their style of play.

Hugo Meisl was the manager and, as we have established, his preferred style was heavily laden with technique and possession rather than brute force and rushing the opposition goal. The city of Vienna provided the perfect canvas for Meisl to implement this style. The mix of culture from the fans and the coffee houses. The willingness of players, fans and coaches to encourage, engage and participate in the styles and ethics of the 'Danubian School'.

This environment diverted football fully down the path of tactical intuition rather than 'hacking'. In Willy Meisl's 1955 book *Soccer Revolution*, he discusses just how important his brother's 'Wunderteam' were to the history of the game and how influential they were going to be for the future of it. The book gives a scathing account of the English game and its missed opportunities in regards to progressing the game they invented. Willy assesses the minutes from the fifth meeting of the Football Association, in 1863. The original rules proposed by the FA included in paragraph ten were as follows: 'If any player shall run with the ball towards the adversaries' goal, any player of the opposite side shall be at liberty to charge, hold, trip or hack him, or wrest the ball from him, but no player shall be held and hacked at the same time.' Willy wrote: 'In the minutes of the fifth meeting they focused mainly on how the Cambridge University rules wished to develop the game by removing hacking from being the main part of the game. In the previous meeting, the FA had decided to swing towards the Cambridge rules. However, during this meeting, the discourse was mainly around how "hacking is the true football game".'[8]

The representatives from Cambridge insisted that, if the FA continued to 'insist on hacking' then the game of football would never develop beyond the 'schoolboys' setting. In the end, compromises were made and the Cambridge rules were implemented, but this original stance has always been deeply rooted in the UK's football DNA. There is a strong argument that there is a connection between the rules covered in paragraph ten of the laws and the 'get stuck in' culture of British football. In the UK, you will still hear it said that foreign players must get used to the pace and physicality of the English game when they arrive to play here and that hard graft and grit win trophies, not 'pretty' football. British football had ignored the work done by Robertson and Hogan in creating a new way of thinking and playing. Now it would miss out on the opportunity to learn from the 'Wunderteam'.

* * *

While 'Wunderteam' is the umbrella term used when referring to the success enjoyed by the Austrian national team in the 1930s, it can be argued that, within the same decade, there were actually two 'Wunderteams'. Hugo Meisl managed both versions and both played what would become the famous pyramid formation (2-3-5), but the only on-pitch footballing influence they shared was that of Matthias Sindelar. The 2-3-5 formation itself was not uncommon, but the way the players interchanged, kept possession and swayed away from the traditions of the game made them stand out. Josef Smistik, an elegant attacking centre-half, would bomb forward, assisting in attack, as well as holding the fort. A role implemented by Hogan at MTK was now becoming an integral part of common systems in football. Once this role was combined with the development of the withdrawn centre-forward in Sindelar, the 'Danubian Whirl' was created. It is fitting that, given the tactical base was influenced heavily by the Scottish passing style, the 'Wunderteam' first earned their iconic nickname after a 5-0 victory over Scotland in 1931. This first version of the 'Wunderteam' would go on to score 44 goals in winning nine and drawing two of their next 11 games, a run which ended with them being recognised as unofficial world champions by winning the second edition of the International Cup (or Švehla Cup, as it became known in honour of the Czechoslovak prime minister who donated the crystal trophy).

The International Cup and club competition the Mitropa Cup were both created through the resourcefulness of Hugo Meisl.[13] The need for clubs and federations to raise funds to support the professional model of the game was the main driver for these competitions. As well as identifying the best national or club sides, the aim was to fill stadiums and create a revenue stream that would filter directly into the coffers of clubs and national federations. In July 1927, both competitions were finalised and became a reality. It was decided that the International Cup would be played over two years, with each participating nation playing each other home and away. The International Cup, which became known as the European Cup in most circles, only featured teams from central Europe because the sceptical Dutch, French, Belgians and British chose not to take part. Italy won the first edition of the tournament, which was held between 1927 and 1930.

Austria and Czechoslovakia came joint second, with Hungary and Switzerland making up the rest of the league. Political relations between Italy and Austria were frail after the Great War and now a fierce rivalry was starting to emerge in football. Meisl was good friends with Vittorio Pozzo, the legendary coach who was in charge of Italy during this period, and they would often discuss tactics and developments in the game. It was no surprise that the two created the best international sides of the era, creating one of the most influential rivalries. The second edition of the International Cup began in 1931 and finished in 1932, featuring the same five teams as the inaugural edition. Due to the strength of the 'Danubian School' nations and that of the Italians, a clear favourite could not be singled out. However, the most bitter rivalry was certainly between the Italians and Austrians and the opening game of the tournament between them at the San Siro in Milan was played in front of 45,000 spectators. Although Italy had won the first International Cup, they had lost both games to the Austrians. This time, Pozzo finally got one over his friend Meisl, winning 2-1, and said: 'I feel like crying. We did it this time. We beat the unbeatable Austria after 20 years. We achieved the feat that had been attempted in vain by four generations of our best players.'[13]

Pozzo is a revolutionary in his own right, with a fantastic back story, but in terms of our quest to unearth the roots of Total Football, he can be regarded as the villain in much the same way as José Mourinho would be to Pep Guardiola's Barcelona, the West Germans were to the Dutch and Sir Alex Ferguson was to Arsène Wenger's Arsenal. Despite their opening defeat by Italy, the Austrians stuck to their guns and the 'Whirl' began to spin European football into a daze. But it needed a kick-start.

Following a 2-1 victory over Czechoslovakia, Austria played out a boring 0-0 draw against Hungary in Vienna. It was a dull affair that prompted the coffee houses to react; the press began to demand an explanation from Meisl as to why Sindelar was not in the starting XI. Without Sindelar, there would have been no 'Whirl' or 'Wunderteam'. His importance became clear to Meisl after he was finally selected for a friendly against Scotland in Vienna on 16 May 1931. Austria won 5-0, inflicting Scotland's first defeat on the continent, and the 'Wunderteam' nickname was coined. Sindelar followed up his brilliant performance against the Scots by proving he was an integral part of the team as they humiliated Germany in two friendly matches before the next International Cup match.

Drawing against Hungary 2-2 in Budapest was not the greatest result on Austria's return to competitive action, but the performance was there. This fed into the next game against Switzerland which ended in an 8-1 victory and set up a mouth-watering home encounter with Italy. In the lead-up to the game, the press focused heavily on the political rivalry between the nations and the 63,000 spectators whistled and heckled as the Italians gave the fascist salute before kick-off. In footballing terms, the press built up the clash of the two biggest stars in the game at the time – Sindelar and Giuseppe Meazza.

The game lived up to the pre-match hype. Austria won 2-1, with Sindelar scoring twice before Meazza pulled one back for Italy. With two games left to play, the trophy was going to be won by either Austrians or Italy. Pozzo's team drew 1-1 with Hungary, but Austria failed to take advantage, also drawing 1-1 in Prague. On the final matchday, something remarkable happened. The 'Whirl' and the 'Wunderteam' had developed through the tournament, but the spirit of 'Scheiberspiel' had never diminished. Austria hosted Switzerland in the final game of the campaign, winning 3-1, and Czechoslovakia's 2-1 victory over Italy in Prague meant Austria had won the International Cup. However, the Viennese fans were disgusted by their team's performance and the coffee houses and newspapers were filled with scathing criticism. The *Neue Freie Presse* newspaper described it as 'a victory too small for 55,000 spectators'. *Das Kleine Blatt* stated that the fans' dissatisfaction was aimed at Meisl, not the players, while another newspaper criticised the team's fitness levels.[13] The Viennese had developed a taste for football that went much further than simply the result of a game.

Even Meisl admitted his team had had a bad day. They may have won the trophy, but the Austrians were not happy unless the brand of football matched their expectations. Elsewhere in the world, however, their success was being recognised and England invited the 'Wunderteam' to play a friendly the following year. Such invitations to continental teams were uncommon at the time, but the English clearly saw the Austrians as worthy challengers to their self-proclaimed dominance.

This was the Austrians' chance to showcase their talents, a chance for the British to take notice, the same opportunity the Hungarians had already given them and would give them again 17 years later. For Austria, the build-up to the game in London was far from perfect, nerves seemingly forming within the camp. Sindelar had been suffering from illness and injuries to Adolf Vogl and Friedrich Gschweidl meant the two were doubtful for the game. Perhaps fittingly, given John Tait Robertson's connections to Chelsea and the 'Danubian School', the match was to be staged at Stamford Bridge.

A crowd of 42,000 were treated to what would become a legendary game. The Austrians began as those who followed them expected, dominating the ball with some impressive passing play, and only poor finishing prevented them taking the lead. It was England who were more clinical, going 2-0 up thanks to a brace from Jimmy Hampson. Going into the second half at 2-0 down, Austria needed a fast start and it came thanks to a goal from a fluent move featuring some great combination play from Sindelar and Anton Schall and finished off by Karl Zischek. This set up a fantastic battle, which had the full attention of the fans. Austria mounted a heap of pressure on the English goal but lacked that decisive finish. England scored a third in the 77th minute, but Austria refused to admit defeat. Sindelar got on the scoresheet only for Sammy Crooks to reply straight away and make it 4-2. The England players were being spun around by the Austrians' neat passing lanes and habit of dropping back behind the ball when out of possession. Austria dominated the game but not the scoreline. Zischek managed a late goal but it wasn't enough to avoid defeat, England winning 4-3.

* * *

This was perhaps the first of many famous games in which a team displaying a style linked to Total Football would make a huge impact despite losing. Unbeknown to the masses of English fans in the stadium, this was 'Scheiberspiel'; for many Austrians, the nature of their team's performance would have felt like a victory. The opposing football philosophies in England and Austria were emphasised two years later when Austria again travelled to London, this time losing 4-2 to Arsenal at Highbury.

Roland Allen reported in the *Evening Standard*: 'It looks fine, it is fine: when the Austrians have learned how to turn all their cleverness into something that counts: when ... they have organised the winning of football matches as highly as they have organised the taming of a football, they will make [everyone] sit up and take notice.' In England, rather than acknowledging that Austrian football was superior, the two defeats were seen as confirmation that teams can play all the passing football they want but that, without scoring goals and winning, it means nothing. The games also fed into the notion in Britain that continental teams lacked punch in the final third. However, when you look at the goalscorers in the Stamford Bridge game, Austrian pair Matthias Sindelar and Karl Zischek became football legends while England's two-goal Jimmy Hampson never played for his country again.

Meisl, who had a habit of sometimes having a little too much to say, helped fuel the debate over English ignorance, saying: 'To us middle Europeans, the attacking play of the British professional, seen from an aesthetic point of view, seems rather poor. Such play consists of assigning the job of scoring goals to the centre-forward and the wings, while to the inside-forwards is allotted the task of linking attackers and defenders, and more as half-backs than as attacking players ... The centre-forward, who, among us in Europe, is the leading figure, because of his technical excellence and tactical intelligence, in England limits his activity to exploiting the errors of the opposing defence.' Perhaps not the most humble way to react to defeat, but Meisl's comments did highlight the progression of the game away from the British Isles. The value of the withdrawn centre-forward role was demonstrated by Sindelar in the Austrians' two defeats in England and this should have been a warning to the English; it would be a role that came back to haunt them in the not-so-distant future. To the English, however, they had scored more goals than the Austrians, so everything seemed perfect.

Meisl would get his revenge on England but, for now, he had to concern himself with preparing for the 1934 World Cup.

* * *

I want to pause the timeline here and focus on Sindelar, as it is not just his playing style that can help uncover the roots of Total Football; his personal story is just as evidential. He was known by many nicknames, but perhaps the most fitting was the 'Mozart of football'. Alfred Polgar, one of the main protagonists of the Wiener Moderne culture, was a columnist, theatre critic, writer and, of course, football enthusiast. Of Sindelar, he said: 'He played football as a chess master moves his pawns, with such an extensive vision that he could calculate moves and counter moves in advance, always choosing the best options. He had unparalleled ball control, combined with the ability to set surprise counter-attacks, as well as being unbelievably good at making fun of opponents by feints.' This analysis suggests that Sindelar deserves to be placed in the same bracket as more recent stars who are lauded as being among the greatest of all time.

Sindelar played with his brain before his feet. Like Cruyff. Like Bergkamp.

The Paper Man

Matthias Sindelar was born in Kozlov, a small village in South Moravia, Bohemia. Like many working class families from Moravia, the Sindelars relocated closer to the imperial capital in search of a better life. Moving in 1905, they settled in Favoriten, a suburb in the south of Vienna. This area was populated with thousands of families who had followed the same journey. Sindelar had plenty of children to play football in the streets with and this is where he began to develop his extraordinary talent. Not in a summer coaching camp, not from being coached one-on-one by his elders, but by playing in the streets with his peers. The football they used would be handmade, of course, from a bundle of old rags tied together.

Sindelar, malnourished and weak, appeared nothing like an athlete, an image he kept throughout his career. The genius of the 'Paper Man' was built on brains, agility and refinement. As with the grunds of Budapest, trainers from clubs in and around Vienna would look out for talented kids playing in the streets, car parks or gardens. Sindelar, it is said, was known to many clubs but wasn't snapped up until his local club, Hertha Vienna, held trials for the local schoolchildren in a bid to turn around a recent run of dire results. In 1918, 15-year-old Sindelar signed his first contract. At this point, Sindelar was an apprentice blacksmith, a job he began at the tender age of 14. His father had died in 1917 and it was up to Matthias to step up and help his mother with raising himself and his three sisters.

In 1921, Sindelar made his first-team debut although his early career was interrupted by injuries. After Hertha were relegated to the Second Division in 1924, they fell into financial difficulties and this led to Sindelar being sold to FK Austria Vienna. National manager Hugo Meisl had been monitoring the player for some years, the only concerns surrounding his fitness, as he had had several knee injuries. Soon after arriving at FK, it was decided by the club doctor and vice chairman Emanuel Schwarz that Sindelar needed knee surgery. It was a successful operation but the 'Paper Man' would sport a knee bandage while playing, a trademark that can be seen in many images taken during his career.

Sindelar won eight trophies in his 15 years with FK, remaining with the club for the rest of his career. In his first full season, he helped the club win the league title. He was the main man at the main club in Vienna and became the hero of the city. The coffee shops were filled with chatter surrounding the 'Mozart of football'. Sindelar loved the accolades he received from the football fans in the city but it was only a matter of time before his name began to ring bells around the continent.

The Mitropa Cup was in full swing by the 1930s. Essentially, it was the first version of the European Cup which would eventually become the Champions League. To begin with, it was exclusively for teams within the Austro-Hungarian empire but, much like the International Cup, it ended up being contested by teams from Czechoslovakia, Italy, Hungary and Austria. In 1933, Austria Vienna would claim their first Mitropa title. Considering this was the most prestigious trophy available to clubs at that time, this highlights the influence of the 'Paper Man'. It was, in fact, during this campaign that Sindelar was first dubbed 'Der Papierene', his performances in the Mitropa Cup attracting comments on his style of play from journalists across Europe.

There are two theories behind the nickname. One is that an Austrian fan came up with it after observing that Sindelar often spent a lot of time laying injured on the ground during matches in a mark of his fragility. The second is that Hugo Meisl coined the nickname in praise of the player's agile and graceful style.

Sindelar was fast becoming a continental icon and many writers, fans and officials considered him the outstanding player of the time. The great Giuseppe Meazza was one of the other names on everyone's lips. Meazza is, perhaps, the more famous name in more recent times but I guess that depends on where you acquire your footballing knowledge. It was a topic which was furiously debated in the 1930s, the nationality of those writing the articles tending to influence who came out on top.

Not long after their battle in the final of the International Cup, the final of the Mitropa Cup in 1933 would be Sindelar v Meazza once again. Ambrosiana Inter, who would later become Inter Milan, were the club of Meazza and, during his first spell there, he would score 240 goals in 348 games. The final was to be played across two legs, just as all other ties in the tournament were. Ambrosiana won the first leg at their ground in Milan, the Arena Civica, in front of 35,000 fans. Ambrosiana won 2-1 and, while there were no goals for Sindelar, Meazza opened the scoring for his side. To sum up the journalistic divide over the relative merits of Sindelar and Meazza, which was similar to the modern day Messi–Ronaldo debate, Luigi Cavallero, a famous Italian journalist with *La Stampa*, wrote after this first leg: 'Anyone who has waited for this match to make a comparison between the two men competing for the international best player palm will surely have been disappointed. How can you judge two players so different? Meazza is cunning, virtuous and skilful, while Sindelar is impetuous and determined … But we can say with our eyes closed that Meazza's class exceeds Sindelar's, beyond what is said in Vienna, where the top player of the "Wunderteam" is considered the champion par excellence.'

The second leg, which took place a week later, was played at Praterstadion in Vienna in front of 60,000 fans and Austria Vienna were crowned champions after a 3-1 win gave them a 4-3 aggregate success. Sindelar scored a hat-trick and, for many, this cemented him as the greatest player in the world. Sindelar was not only receiving plaudits from journalists, in the coffee houses and on the terraces, but his opponents were also beginning to recognise his excellence. Sindelar had become the symbol of FK Austria Vienna; the club's links to the liberal Jewish and Bohemian life and their relationship with the coffee houses of Vienna meant that it was a club which belonged to Sindelar as much as he belonged to it. Transfer approaches were frequent.

Rapid offered 35m crowns and bids also came from England, with Arsenal prepared to pay £40,000 and Charlton Athletic expressing their interest in the forward. Slavia Prague also attempted to replace the legendary František Svoboda with the 'Paper Man'. The sums of money being offered would have been almost impossible to turn down because of the financial situation FK, like many other clubs at the time, faced.

Sindelar refused every offer; he loved playing for FK and would become an icon and the most popular player in the history of the club. The first idol hailing from the 'Viennese School' was Josef Uridil, whose story was similar to Sindelar's but the 'Paper Man' would surpass the fame of 'the Tank'. In terms of representing 'Scheiberspiel', there was no one more fitting than Sindelar. 'He read the game as the actors interpreted their scripts, directed his team as the greatest composers of classical music conducted their orchestras and wrote drafts and stories on the field just as literary celebrities did in Vienna's coffee houses.' This passage from a chronicle based in Vienna helps paint a picture of how Sindelar played and how he influenced those who watched him. As the 'Wunderteam' began to hit the heights, Sindelar would now start to be recognised as the nation's top talent. As a result of a dispute between Sindelar and Meisl, Sindelar's international career never really took off until 1931. After his debut in 1926, in which he scored, he was only called up once between 1928 and 1931.

His performance against Scotland in 1931 established him in the team and, while the game signalled that the 'Wunderteam' as a whole were moving to a new level, it is important to focus in on Sindelar in particular. His personality helps form a greater understanding of what a 'Total Footballer' would one day look like. After that sublime performance against the Scots, the 'Wunderteam' went on an 11-game unbeaten run, winning nine and drawing two, and central to the discussions in the Austrian press and in the coffee houses was Sindelar. On the field, his unpredictable style, his dummies and feints continually bamboozled defenders. Off the field, his fame grew and grew. He featured in a film, *Roxy und das Wunderteam*, and was chosen to endorse products including wristwatches and dairy produce. Despite all this fame, Sindelar remained grounded, just as Uridil had. He didn't get too big for his boots and remained true to his profession and to the ethics of his city. Sindelar never declared public support for any political party although he never hid his social democratic leanings.

Sindelar was shy, a man of very few words. He was a chain smoker, but not a drinker. While crisis and discontent were brewing in Vienna, football remained at the forefront of the city's reputation; they were now recognised as pioneers and Sindelar was loved by all. Sindelar, who did not particularly enjoy the limelight, held together the city by playing the game he loved. Despite the trouble brewing in Vienna, the people had their football and it was very much their own; a brand of football created and allowed to grow in Vienna, assisted by the talents of Sindelar. The 1931/32 International Cup triumph owed much to Sindelar's contribution even though he only became a regular starter after the Scotland game.

* * *

In April 1932, Austria won 8-2 in a friendly against Hungary, with Sindelar giving a performance written into the history books as his most impressive ever. He scored his second hat-trick for his country and his form appeared to be peaking at the perfect time ahead of the 1934 World Cup. Austria went into the second edition of the tournament, hosted by Italy, as big favourites. Austria Vienna had just won the Mitropa Cup and the World Cup fell in the middle of the latest International Cup competition in which Austria had just defeated front-runners Italy 4-2 and had games in hand on them. For World Cup hosts Italy, however, failure on home soil was not an option given the expectations of ruler Benito Mussolini and their fierce rivalry with Austria.

Before the finals, Jules Rimet claimed Italy's motivation to prevail over all others as hosts made them favourites. However, he believed Austria posed their biggest threat, saying: 'The virtues of the Austrians have no equal throughout the continent.' Illustrating the success of the 'Danubian School', Hungary were also among the favourites and boasted a new batch of stars. These included Gyorgy Sarosi and players from the highly successful Hungarian club side Újpest. Hungary captain László Sternberg was a stubborn defender, while Istvan Avar was a prolific goalscorer. Another key player was Istvan Palotas, a striker for the famous MTK. Many historians and football writers have credited Palotas with being the pioneer of the withdrawn centre-forward role in the Hungary team, years before Nandor Hidegkuti made it famous. Palotas had the ability to break away from his position leading the line and drop back into the space, creating gaps for runners and helping him create goals for his team-mates. Another team who entered the finals with high expectations were Czechoslovakia. They boasted some top talent such as the legendary goalkeeper František Plánička, Antonín Puč, the greatest goalscorer of all time for the Czechoslovak national team, and 'Olda' Nejedlý, who would end the tournament as top scorer.

Despite the stiff competition, the Italians fancied their chances and certainly had a strong squad. They had a great goalkeeper in Gianpiero Combi. In defence, Italy could call on Luis Monti, a hard, ruthless tackler who could also pass the ball and read the game. Monti was the perfect fit in the 2-3-2-3 formation or 'Metodo' devised by manager Pozzo. It was, in fact, a system which had many of the 'Danubian School' factors built into it and was a transformation of the more common 2-3-5 pyramid formation. Pozzo knew his players would need more support in the midfield against better opponents and chose to pull back two forwards to sit in front of the midfield. Pozzo was an early advocate of man-marking and his sides were built on solidity and passion. The golden boy of the team was, of course, Meazza. Like the Hungarian forward Palotas, his ability to drop deep meant he was just as adept at creating goals as scoring them.

Austria, though, were the team everyone feared. Manager Meisl believed World Cup victory would be a fitting reward for the style and brand of football the Austrians had developed since the end of the Great War and he was desperate not to fall short. He wanted to appoint his old pal Jimmy Hogan once again to ensure the title was won, but financial constraints meant the Englishman was unable to join up with the coaching team. Franz Hansl was hired instead and, as a former Torino, Alessandria, Livorno and Salernitana manager, he knew the Italian game well. This gave Meisl more confident of beating his biggest rivals, but the 1934 World Cup would be another case of an innovative, entertaining style of football falling short of the major prize.

Austria's first game was against France and the 'Wunderteam' struggled to impose their free-flowing, attacking style. France took the lead and, in boiling conditions in Turin, looked the more likely team to progress to the next round and were unlucky not to extend their lead. However, when French defender Étienne Mattler made a dreadful mistake, the 'Paper Man' took advantage to score the equalizer and the game ended 1-1 after 90 minutes. It was only in extra time that the Austrians' talent began to shine through. Perhaps it was nerves? Austria scored two goals through Anton Schall and Josef Bican before France added a penalty five minutes from the end.

This set up a mouthwatering tie between Austria and Hungary in the quarter-finals. The Danube derby, to be played in Bologna, would see two similar teams going head-to-head, two teams who would be pushing for goals and victory throughout. Both countries had absorbed the influence of the Scottish passing game and developed themselves into something unique and debate raged as to which of these two central European teams were the best. For many, this game answered that question. The 'Wunderteam' won 2-1 and proved that, for now, they had something more than the Hungarians. Austria's win propelled them into the semi-finals, where they would have to see off another great rival – hosts Italy.

If the game against Hungary was seen as two brothers fighting, this game was the opposite. Bitter rivals, not just on the football pitch but on the battlefield, with memories of the First World War still fresh. It was once again Meazza v Sindelar, although the two men had become good friends on the back of the rivalry that was often played out in the media as much as on the pitch. But, for this game, there was no room for friendship. Mussolini was in the crowd and, for him, losing this game could not be contemplated. The match pitched a nationalistic, man-marking steamroller against the expressive art of free-flowing Danubian football. The game was regarded by many as the real final and, although a record San Siro crowd of 40,000 watched the game, the stadium was really too small to host such a spectacle.

On 3 June 1934, Austria took on Italy for a place in the World Cup Final. It was the opportunity for Meisl and his Austrian team to secure their place in the history books. The pitch at the San Siro would not have been passed fit for a Sunday league game today, never mind a World Cup semi-final; it was a boggy field with patches of sand covering much of it. The Italians took an early lead through Enrique Guaita after a heavy challenge from Meazza on the Austrian goalkeeper Peter Platzer forced him to fumble a low cross.

It was surprising that Swedish referee Ivan Eklind allowed Meazza's challenge on Platzer and the officiating would follow this path throughout, with a clear leniency towards the Italians. Sindelar was having his typically graceful impact on the game, linking up play well, dropping into the space that he had made his own. Luis Monti, Sindelar's old foe from the 1933/34 Mitropa Cup, would take matters into his own hands. Monti was permitted to get away with a series of bad challenges and Italian manager Pozzo, writing later in *La Stampa*, said of the clashes between Sindelar and Monti: 'They didn't get along at all. It was mutual. It was one of those natural, instinctive, irresistible antipathies. The Viennese did not like Luisisto's [Monti's] resolute, masculine character and Luisisto did not like the dances of the Austrian, who seemed to want to make fun of him.' Pozzo was applauding thuggery over trickery and elegance. Sindelar was not trying to make fun of his opponents, he was simply playing the game the way best suited not only to his talent but his physique. Pozzo finished his piece in *La Stampa* with comments about how Monti's unpopularity was mainly due to criticism he received from kicking down an idol like Sindelar – the same type of bitterness we see nowadays when someone does not appreciate the beauty of the football and can only see the game as something that must be won.

The Austrians had four good chances to equalise before half-time but Combi was guarding his goal just like the many great Italian goalkeepers who would follow in his footsteps. When the teams came out for the second half, Sindelar was almost out of gas after his battle with Monti. The second half was dominated by caution and there were few clear chances. Austria's best opportunity came right at the end of the game, but Zischek's effort was off target. Italy were through to the final while Austria had to make do with the third-place play-off against Germany. Eklind went on to referee the final between Italy and Czechoslovakia, an appointment he was said to have been promised by Mussolini himself ahead of the crunch semi-final and, after the hosts won 2-1 after extra time, the Czechs complained that the referee's performance was suspicious to say the least.

Meisl, assessing how his Austrian team's wonderful run of results had been ended by the Italians, said: 'It happened exactly as I imagined. It was impossible to beat Italy in such a context. You have to surrender the title to the Azzurri. But that does not mean that their football is better and that the title was won deservedly.' These comments may sound bitter and I am sure they were coloured by the disappointment Meisl felt at suffering defeat in his biggest game as a coach, but his words could also fit other big games in which a superior style of football has failed to yield a victory. Does this mean styles of football such as that displayed by the 'Wunderteam' are historically unsuccessful and do not deserve a place at the table alongside those of winning teams? In this case, the reasons for Austria's defeat went beyond football.

Italian player Raimundo Orsi was later quoted as claiming the players would have been in danger of the death penalty if Eklind had not been on their side that day.[13] Austrian player Bican commented: 'We knew that the referee was corrupt and that he would arbitrate in favour of Italy. He even went as far as to play with them; at one point we passed the ball to the right wing and one of my team-mates, Zischek, ran to reach it, but the referee returned it to the Italians. It was a disgrace.' These comments cannot disguise the fact that Italy probably deserved to win – throughout the match, they created the better chances and they defended well –

but they do give a little more insight into how the game was shaped. The manner of Italy's victory also highlights the respect opponents had for the 'Whirl'; rather than trying to compete with the Austrians at their own game, teams simply tried to stop them playing. As would be the case with the Hungarians and the Dutch at future World Cups, a revolutionary style of football did not claim the ultimate prize. However, it was clear that the Austrians had put their stamp on the blueprint for Total Football.

The Austrians were defeated again in the play-off against Germany and the 'Wunderteam' looked nothing like the side who had earned that nickname. Sindelar did not take part; he was exhausted and injured after his battle with Monti. The game took place in Naples at the Municipal Stadium and only around 9,000 people attended, no doubt adding to Meisl's feelings of sorrow, as it had been more than 15 years since his side played in front of so few spectators.

The players looked tired and conceded after only 25 seconds on their way to a 3-2 defeat. Widespread criticism after the World Cup saw the players accused of being in poor physical condition, training methods and player nutrition were called into question and much of the flak was aimed towards Meisl. Over a 15-year period, Meisl had managed to transform the nation's football team and culture, developing a style of play which reflected the coach's personality and beliefs, but defeat at the World Cup signalled the beginning of the end for his great Austrian side. The team did continue to perform for a number of years, but they would not get the chance of revenge over Italy on the World Cup stage in 1938 as the years leading up to it would be damning for the nation as a whole.

The death of the 'Wunderteam'

Hugo Meisl was not showing any signs of slowing down his drive to build and grow the game. He was in the middle of forming a third wave of 'Wunderteam'. In 1936, Meisl finally enjoyed a victory over England as Austria beat them 2-1 in Vienna. The English found the warm conditions too much for their manic kick-and-rush style and the possession-based play of the Austrians was far better suited under the hot sun in the Austrian capital. Sindelar repeatedly dragged John Barker out of position and all over the pitch, just as Hungary's Nandor Hidegkuti would do to England centre-half Harry Johnston 17 years later, the technical excellence and tactical intelligence of a centre-forward embarrassing a nation so proud of their punch in the final third. England's Jack Crayston commented: 'We didn't know whether we were coming or going.' It was another unheeded warning to England, another unfulfilled chance to embrace this new style of play and build around it.

On 17 February 1937, Hugo Meisl passed away from a heart attack at the age of 55. Although his death came as a major shock at the time, Meisl had suffered from heart problems earlier in his life. A man who devoted almost all of his life to developing not only Austrian football but the game of football as a whole died whilst carrying out interviews with a promising young First Vienna player called Richard Fischer. Meisl wanted reassurances over the player's age because, although Fischer claimed to be only 17, Meisl was aware of him having been described several years earlier as a promising 17-year-old.

It is believed that Meisl entered the room, acknowledged Fischer, sat down and immediately collapsed. Austria Vienna president Emanuel Schwarz, a doctor and lifelong friend of

Meisl's, was called instantly but all he could do was confirm the cause of death.

Condolences flooded in from around the world. Richard Eberstaller, president of the ÖFB (Austrian FA), commented: 'At the moment it is impossible for us to estimate the weight of this loss, but the merits of Meisl remain immense. He has represented the essence of the enthusiasm that has been created for football, not only in us but all over the world. As the great professional he was, he was able to bring all his expertise to football.' Eberstaller said the 'entire football community' was in mourning. His statement provides evidence of just how instrumental Meisl was in shaping the game of football as a whole and it is interesting that the comments focus on his character and how it sat so well with the passion that was growing for football. No matter what playing style or trend you want to focus on, it would be hard not to trace it back to Meisl in some capacity. There is a room at the museum of Austria Vienna that is dedicated to the life of Hugo Meisl.

If there was a museum devoted to the world of football, I am sure Meisl would feature at the heart of it. A man who was willing to engage in new ideas and progress tactics and strategies that were created by others, Meisl had the drive and determination to make them work for him; all of this while, most importantly, staying true to what he believed in and thought was best for the game he loved.

As war became increasingly inevitable, the 'Wunderteam' would find itself dismantled. On 15 March 1938, at the Neue Hofburg on Heldenplatz in front of around 250,000 people, Adolf Hitler delivered his speech making the annexation of Austria official. For Austrian football this meant a return to amateur status. Austrian teams withdrew from the Mitropa

Cup and the International Cup was suspended. The Nazis had destroyed Meisl's work over the past 15 years in a matter of hours.

Less than a month after the annexation, it was announced that the German and Austrian football associations were to merge. To mark this, a friendly was organised between the two national sides. German coach Sepp Herberger regarded the merger as a chance to tap into the great 'Wunderteam' in a bid to create the ideal team to challenge for the 1938 World Cup in France by mixing the physical players of Germany with the technical players of the Austrians. The German coach was studying in Berlin in 1930 when he wrote a thesis on the importance of combination football and the passing game, so he seemed like the perfect man to merge two styles and create a new version of the 'Wunderteam'. Herberger – who joined the Nazi Party in 1933 and was given the German national team job in 1936 after four years as assistant coach – is an important name for us to discuss. He was maybe one of Total Football's nemeses during the early years of its development, but it also has to be considered whether he actually contributed to its creation by attempting to halt its development?

The Germany–Austria friendly international took place on 3 April 1938 and was dubbed by the Germans the 'Anschlussspiel game' in a reference to the Nazis' term celebrating Austria's return to the Reich. Some of the Austrian players regarded the game as an opportunity to go from the declining 'Wunderteam' into the Germany team and earn a chance of playing at the World Cup. For others, the game was more about patriotism and a chance to show that Austrian football was still the best. The match took place at the Vienna Prater Stadium in front of 60,000 people including members of the Nazi hierarchy. Despite rumours that circulated for many years afterwards, Hitler was not in attendance. The venue resembled one in Berlin rather than Vienna, with the stadium draped in swastika flags. This game has been reported on numerous times over the years, with a focus on Sindelar's blatant disrespect towards the Nazi regime.

It has been reported that it was Sindelar's decision for the team to play in red. This was not the case, as Jo Araf summarises in *Generazione Wunderteam*. After a goalless first half, Sindelar broke the deadlock with a trademark striker's finish from inside the penalty area. Some reports have described it as a 30-yard wonder goal followed by a huge celebration by the 'Paper Man' in front of the Nazi hierarchy. Again, as Jo Araf explains in *Generazione Wunderteam*, this is incorrect on both counts. Sindelar's goal celebration was nothing more exaggerated than usual and if he was celebrating in front of anyone, it would have been 100 or so Austria fans who were in the grandstand near the Nazi bigwigs, as Sindelar knew this would be his last international appearance before his adoring public. The lead was doubled when Karl Sesta scored from about 30 yards. At the end of the game, medals and prizes were handed out. It has been reported that the only players not to take part in the Nazi salute were Sindelar and Sesta.

It has also been claimed that Sesta served two weeks in prison as a result. However, there is no evidence, photographically or in print, to support any of this. What is clear is that Sindelar played his trademark elegant football in this game and yet, as evidence of his beliefs and character, he was the only one of the 22 players on the park who would never play for Germany. Seven of the Austrian XI went on to represent the Germans at the World Cup while the others played in friendlies or other representative matches.

With Austrian football no long professional, players had to look for other ways to earn a living. Sindelar, fittingly given his influence on 'Scheiberspiel', bought the Annahof, a coffee house slap bang in the middle of Favoriten, the neighbourhood where he was brought up. Sindelar had no motivation to play the game at the level Austrian football now found itself at, so he retired. What was so unique about Sindelar was that he never left his city. He was clever with his investments and the purchase of the coffee shop and a grocery store, alongside a role as a manager at a local sports goods company, meant the transition to life after football was a smooth one.

Among the many myths surrounding Sindelar were reports that he was Jewish. This perhaps sprung from his unbreakable relationship with FK Austria, who had strong Jewish roots. On the evening of 22 January 1939, Sindelar and close friend Egon Ulbrich, the FK manager, met up with other friends at the Cafe Weidinger for a typical night out. Ulbrich recalled: 'We played [cards] and drank all night.' Afterwards, Sindelar headed to an apartment along Annagasse where his girlfriend, Camilla Castagnola, lived.

The next morning, Sindelar and Camilla were found dead. The death of the city's hero sparked widespread rumours. Was it suicide? Murder? Some claimed the Gestapo had been investigating whether Sindelar was Jewish and had killed the couple. Some people linked the deaths to Sindelar's alleged behaviour in the Anschlussspiel game, but we now know that those events appear to have been fabricated. Lurid rumours also spread about Camilla. Some alleged that she was a prostitute, while others claimed she was a target for the

Gestapo because she was an Italian-Jewish immigrant who had supported the Fascist Party until 1938. It is believed now that Camilla was, in fact, born in Austria and inherited her Italian surname after marrying an Italian, Mario Castagnola.

An autopsy carried out by Dr Schneider on 26 January concluded that the cause of death was carbon monoxide inhalation intoxication. Poisoning was categorically disregarded. The Gestapo investigators who attended the scene spoke to neighbours who commented that the stove had been emitting smoke and gas for days. The many rumours and myths surrounding Sindelar's death only go to illustrate what an influential figure he had become in Vienna and the impact the game of football had on the city and its inhabitants.

Friedrich Torberg and Alfred Polgar, two men whose opinions were held in the highest regard by the intellectuals of Vienna at the time, both wrote that they believed Sindelar had committed suicide because he could no longer bear to live under barbaric Nazi rule in the city he loved. Polgar wrote: 'The good Sindelar did not detach himself from the city of which he was the son and pride until his death. Everything leads us to think of a death caused by his loyalty to his country. To live and play football in such a tormented, destroyed and oppressed city would have meant betraying it. How could you play under such conditions? Or to live, when a life without football is nothing?'

What cannot be denied is the impact Sindelar had on the world of football. He was perhaps the first player to make the game look like an art form. Sindelar, to many Viennese, is the hero the city needed to represent its core values. He was a man who never denied his origins, despite being the talk of the streets and the bourgeois coffee houses. As Torberg put it: 'Sindelar was loved by every Viennese who knew him; in other words he was loved by everyone.'

As with other Total Football luminaries, tales and myths grew around Sindelar which were not necessarily a true reflection of his character. He was often described as an introvert whose personality would certainly not light up the room. However, due to his ability on the football field, a character has been formed to whom we can all relate. When we think of our favourite players, we often craft in our own minds how, from what we see on the field, their personality away from football would be. In Sindelar's era, the 'Danubian School' and 'Scheiberspiel' were not only impacting football tactics and results, they were shaping people's imaginations and their views on society as a whole.

Sepp Herberger has already been mentioned as having perhaps been a nemesis of the style of play this book is trying to capture, but, leading up to the 1938 World Cup, he was facing a number of questions around which style of play he was going to implement.

Still relatively young and with great pressure on his shoulders, the decision he had to make was one that every coach must face at some point in their career. What style of football do I believe in? How do I want my team to play? What will bring me success? Herberger's dilemma was even more fascinating as he had the choice of two styles, two cultures and two sets of players. Would he go for Hugo Meisl's 'Viennese Whirl' or the more regimented W-M the Germans were accustomed to? A style built on strength and athleticism, which was rooted very firmly in the German mentality, or the 'Scheiberspiel' which gave players more freedom to express themselves and use a short-passing, possession-based style? Would Herberger like his team to entertain or would he build a disciplined team fixated only on winning?

It wasn't just at international level that Austrian football was forced into a union with the Germans; domestically, Austrian teams began to play in the German league and the two contrasting playing styles would constantly clash. As preparations for the 1938 World Cup intensified, it was now apparent which formation Herberger was going to use. He was one of the first to move away from the W-M formation, opting for the 2-3-5 of the 'Whirl'. This would act as a spur for many German teams to follow suit.

Although Herberger did not have Sindelar, there was much anticipation surrounding the German squad, bolstered by recruits from Austria's 'Wunderteam', when they arrived in France for the World Cup finals. With the tournament staged on a knockout basis, Germany were drawn against Switzerland. After a 1-1 draw at the Parc des Princes in Paris on 4 June, the replay took place at the same ground on 8 June in front of a rowdy French crowd who hurled objects on to the pitch in protest at neighbours Germany (at this point, war was only 18 months away). Germany were hopeless, losing 4-2. When they made a fast start and took the lead, it briefly looked like being the start of something special, but that did not last long. Herberger was furious and, whether it is what he actually believed or if he was just trying to save face and pass the buck, he blamed the Austrian players for costing his team the game, claiming they did not fully engage with the strict discipline he was trying to enforce. For many observers, it was the clash of football cultures that caused Germany's downfall.

No matter how Herberger decided to play or which of the two football cultures he attempted to promote above the other, it was clear that the Germans and Austrians were on a different page to each other and it was this disjointedness that held back the team. Although the Austrian dream had died, the 1938 final did include another team from the 'Danubian School', with Hungary making it through to play Pozzo's Italy, who lifted the trophy for a second successive World Cup. Although the Hungarians had faded slightly by 1938, the football they had built and spread to Austria was now going to make its way across the world. The Hungarian influence on the blueprint of how the game should be played would never be removed and arguably their influence on Italian football would hold the most weight and is often overlooked. More than 60 of the coaches working in Italian football during the years 1920–45 would be of Hungarian origin and there is no doubt most of, if not all of them, would have been disciples of the game Jimmy Hogan and John Tait Robertson brought to their country.

The example of Germany's failure in 1938, when they attempted to mix 'Scheiberspiel' with a more regimented and disciplined style, helps tackle a recurring question relating to Total Football. It is often said that when the Netherlands lost to West Germany in the 1974 World Cup Final, despite being the best team in the tournament, they would surely have won had they played in a more conventional, disciplined style for at least part of the final. When one considers the example of Germany in 1938, my answer would be 'no'. Germany's failure proved that you can't make these styles work together. Discipline in the 'Whirl', for example, was to pass the ball quickly and effectively and interchange with your team-mates. Discipline in a 4-4-2 formation is the two banks of four in defence and midfield. A football team's success is centred around the quality of players in that team.

The way they play or the culture behind their style is often the side dish and, as we begin to look at River Plate's 'La Maquina' team, this will add another element to this picture and again help us understand the next building block on the road to Total Football.

Whereas the Hungarians were a blank canvas and it is easier to piece together exactly where their inspiration came from, this style of football was now becoming far more complex. The Austrians certainly brought a more individual feeling to the style, not just in terms of how they played but also the people who enjoyed it. The coffee houses being so integral in the performances on the pitch help prove this perhaps more than anything else and it was this part of society that really drove and shaped the great 'Wunderteam'. In relation to the modern game, there is nothing one could equate to the coffee house culture. In the UK, pubs are still a place to watch football with friends, strangers and enemies and discourse still takes place as it would have in the coffee houses. But there is a lot more tainting a fan's views now than there was in the 1900s. The internet and, more specifically, social media have played a massive part in this. A 90-minute game is condensed into a ten-second clip and this ten-second clip can be enough to influence someone's beliefs and enjoyment of the game.

The breaking news of a transfer or the behaviour of a player in a nightclub take precedence over analysis and detailed tactical discourse. Although social media does also play a big part in the latter, it is often easier to get your fix from the quick tabloid-like coverage of the game rather than spending ten minutes taking in an article. Scorelines mean more than ever to the fan, as there is usually a bet or fantasy football points (often with money at stake) involved. Much of what analysis there is usually involves over-analysing a 'mistake' from a defender, a five-minute breakdown of a refereeing decision that had no real impact on the game or, even worse, a week-long trial played out over the sports news networks like a criminal court case over whether the video assistant referee got a decision correct. This is solely the view of a fan based in the UK and I must be fair and say there is still some brilliant technical and tactical analysis available, but the headlines will almost always be dominated by the world of breaking news.

The coffee house culture continued its influence into the modern era. Barcelona's famous La Masia academy was situated not far from the Camp Nou when nurturing Xavi, Iniesta, Messi, Busquets and the other great players of that era and it was often referred to as having the same feeling to that of the coffee houses of an earlier generation. Members of the public could walk in, members of the club had a lot of influence on the club's direction and there is no doubt this environment and culture helped shape possibly the greatest club team of its generation and a contender as one of the greatest club teams ever seen. That site is now closed and Barcelona's recent plight at the time of writing this book does not need to be analysed too much, but Barcelona are a million miles away from what they were at the time when Pep Guardiola instilled a style of football which certainly seemed to stem from the Danubian roots of the early 1900s.

The culture and motivation of that Barcelona team had its paws firmly dug into the impact that the football made on those watching and supporting it, just as football in Austria did during the 'Wunderteam' era and you have to wonder if there is room for this type of commitment now in the modern game. Do football clubs need to entertain fans?

Or just please sponsors and executives? Is 'Scheiberspiel' gone forever?

Herbert Chapman

The English game was still strong and England arguably remained the most respected country in terms of football and the innovation of the game. Hugo Meisl's close friend, Herbert Chapman, built a fantastic Arsenal side during the late 1920s and early 1930s and his name is almost always brought up, along with Jimmy Hogan and Meisl, in discussions about the great creators of the modern game. Chapman's playing career took in a number of Football League and non-league clubs and, without him ever reaching the top of the game, he still enjoyed a decent career. But it was through his impact as a coach that he would become a household name, starting out with Northampton Town before moving to Leeds City and Huddersfield Town and then, in 1925, to Arsenal. He was one of the first coaches to really implement tactics and a style of play on his teams. This quote from him sums up his frustrations with English football when he began coaching at Northampton Town: 'No attempt was made to organise victory. The most that I remember was the occasional chat between, say, two men playing on the same wing.'

Chapman no doubt shared many a discussion with his friend Meisl about keeping the ball and the passing game, but he believed that teams could end up extending passages of attacking play for too long, making it easier for teams to defend against them. Chapman began to look at how he could counter this problem and became a revolutionary in trying to create space for his teams to attack. In the 1970s, Rinus Michels and Valeriy Lobanovskyi almost simultaneously became fixated with the idea that football was all about space. Space on the pitch was something that Johan Cruyff was endlessly quoted on. Space was something that the Dutch side of the 1970s built their play on. Finding space, playing into space and creating space. In the book *Herbert Chapman, Football Emperor,* Stephen Studd outlines how Chapman brought his midfield deeper in a ploy to give more space to his attackers by drawing out the opposition's defence and team as a whole, whilst ensuring that his own team built from the back when they had the chance and played between each other when in trouble. Chapman used the traditional 2-3-5 formation at the time (it is important to remember that this was a time during the old offside law) and a sort of planned counter-attacking style.

This is something Total Football is not always related to, but this idea of creating space and how to make it an advantage was certainly part of the blueprint we are trying to uncover. By the time Chapman arrived at Arsenal, he had developed his counter-attacking style and, with the new offside rule being introduced, aimed to take it to a new level. The change in the laws meant an attacker was onside if two opponents, rather than three, were between him and the goal line. To fully take advantage of the new rule, Chapman needed some help. He signed Charlie Buchan, Sunderland's record goalscorer, for £2,000, with Sunderland getting a further £100 every time he scored for his new club.

Buchan consulted with Chapman about an idea he had to move the centre-half from the middle of the park to become a 'stopper' at the centre of the defence. This passed the responsibility for setting an offside trap from the full-backs, the two out-and-out defenders in the 2-3-5 formation, to the centre-half and also meant the full-backs could be positioned wider to cover the wings. Inspired by Buchan's idea, Chapman introduced the W-M or 3-4-3, which would almost become a 3-2-2-3 formation. He withdrew the two inside-forwards, who had typically been part of a front five, to play deeper behind the centre-forward and two wingers. Behind the inside-forwards, two half-backs played in midfield, with the new 'stopper' centre-half at the heart of a three-man defence. This trend was quickly picked up by teams across the British Isles, with Newcastle United, Tottenham Hotspur and Queen's Park all converting to the W-M formation. Chapman, who had already proved his brilliant tactical nous at his previous clubs, didn't just settle with the new formation to exploit the change in the offside rule.

He maximised his counter-attacking style, arming his team with speedy wingers and stubborn defenders. 'The most opportune time for scoring is immediately after repelling an attack, because opponents are then strung out in the wrong half of the field,' Chapman explained during his time as a coach. It is a principle that many modern football styles are built on now, a style that has often proved decisive in the biggest tournaments and a style which is quite possibly the most effective way to suppress the success of the Total Football style, but also arguably a style which shares many of the same ideas. Later, we will see how this style developed further when the great Ernő Egri Erbstein created his famous Torino side of the 1940s. Torino's style is often cited as a predecessor to that of Michels and Cruyff but was built on the foundations Chapman laid.

With the change in the offside law in 1925 and the emergence of a new generation of coaches, the game was growing and new tactics were being formed. As a result, it becomes increasingly tricky to trace the development of the style of play associated with Total Football. However, by studying the development of the game in South America we can uncover another root in the tree that was growing around this style. We will see the importance of patience and developing youth players whilst teaching and implementing a style of play with all the teams associated with a football club at all levels.

Part 3

The South American Machine

FOOTBALL IN Europe was entering a time of uncertainty. After the demise of the 'Wunderteam' and the abysmal performance of Germany at the 1938 World Cup, there was a question mark over what would happen to the 'Danubian School' and the teachings instilled into those who played, coached or watched this style grow and dominate football in the regions it was played in. What must be remembered when trying to plot the journey of Total Football is that it is almost impossible not only to pinpoint exactly what Total Football is but also who actually created it and when it was created.

The origins were certainly rooted in the Scottish passing style and it was not only Jimmy Hogan and John Tait Robertson who were exposed to this and spread the word. At around the time Robertson was beginning his managerial career with Chelsea and Glossop, another Scot was leaving the British Isles to spread his football experiences and beliefs. Although the name John Harley may not have had much significance to football in Scotland or the UK, his impact in South America is hard to beat. Born in Glasgow on 5 May 1886, Harley became a railway worker and, in 1906, travelled to Argentina to work on the Bahia Blanca railway. Although not known for his footballing ability in Scotland, he played for several teams in Argentina before settling for work on the line which would run near the Rio de la Plata, which translates to River Plate, commonly known by football fans as the name of one of Argentina's biggest football clubs. The river forms part of the border between Uruguay and Argentina and both countries would benefit from not only the Scotsman's trade as a railway worker but also from his influence on football. Harley played for Buenos Aires-based Ferro Carril Oeste. The club was founded in 1904 by railway workers, which is most likely the reason Harley ended up playing for them.

But it would be Uruguay who would benefit the most from Harley in these early days of his time in South America, as he moved on to Uruguay to play his football after being scouted by Central Uruguay Railway Cricket Club (CURCC) after they played a friendly against Ferro Carril Oeste in 1908. The Uruguayans offered him a job and a club at which he could play the game he loved. CURCC were founded in Montevideo in 1891 by British workers from the UK company Central Uruguay Railway to play various sports. The club would later become Peñarol when CURCC cut its ties with football.

* * *

In similar fashion to what Robertson, Meisl and Hogan did in Europe – and what Archie McLean was doing in São Paulo, Brazil, at the same time – Harley changed the style of Uruguayan football from the aggressive, long-ball style to a game based on passing and movement. This is another example of the worldwide impact Scots have had on the game. The fact that Uruguay won the first World Cup is always an easy one to answer in a pub quiz, but what might surprise people is that it was a victory engineered by a Scottish railway worker. Although Harley is only recognised as having played and managed the national team of Uruguay for a relatively short period, he succeeded in implementing his style on the country; it would become known as 'corto a pe', which translates as 'short to foot'. Harley was not blessed with height and strength, but he was aggressive and played as a centre-half. Nicknamed 'El Yoni' (Source) of all of their success, Harley is recognised as the country's first tactically minded player. Although born in Scotland, Harley played for Uruguay 17 times between 1909 and 1916 and also captained and managed the side on occasions during this period. He played for Peñarol from 1909 to 1920 and was later their manager. His legacy as Peñarol's number five is still acknowledged by fans of the club to this day and he is buried in the British cemetery in his adopted hometown of Montevideo. He promoted his beliefs and ideas to the national team, helping them win back-to-back Olympic golds in 1924 and 1928 before winning the 1930 World Cup.

All three victories were accomplished using Harley's 'short to foot' style. His personality also fits the mould of the characters already discussed, as he was an ambassador of fair play.

In a game against Central Español Fútbol Club in 1913, Harley deliberately missed a penalty as he believed the referee had made a mistake in awarding his side the foul. Peñarol went on to lose the game 2-1 and this sporting act summed up the centre-back who captained Peñarol and was the symbol of the club in that era. His ability to read the game and the intelligence of his tactics allowed him to stand out across the country and, instead of trying to fight and reject his ideas, the country took note and benefited.

Harley's influence on the Uruguayan international team cannot be disputed. Leading up to the 1930 World Cup, they were already considered to be one of the best teams in the world. Harley's visionary work included tactical insights, new training ideas and the development of players individually. The 1930 World Cup, in which hosts Uruguay beat Argentina in the final, would introduce Carlos Peucelle to the biggest football stage. Peucelle is regarded as one of the earliest prototypes of a Total Footballer and one of the first to grace South American football. It would, of course, be almost 50 years before the term Total Footballer would be created, but it is obvious from descriptions of Peucelle's traits and attributes as a player why these links are often made.

There is no doubt that Harley's influence on South American football spread from Uruguay to Argentina and to the rest of the continent. But what Argentina needed was their own Harley to help develop the game further.

As with all footballing styles, Harley's 'short to foot' would be developed and adapted. It would be a Hungarian who, after landing in South America in 1929, would not only pick up and develop the work of Harley but add what he had learned from the impact Robertson and Hogan had on football in his homeland. He was known as Emérico Hirschl but was born Imre Hirschl. He is a complex character who is difficult to understand, mainly as there are so many different tales surrounding him. Many of these appear to have been created by the man himself, who shared similar character traits with Hogan. What cannot be disputed is that his arrival in Argentinian football coincided with one of their greatest ever club sides being formed. The River Plate team, who would become known as 'La Maquina', shared many similarities to the teams of the 'Danubian School'.

However, when this was mixed with the South American culture, it created a new style with a different edge to the football played in Austria and Hungary. By analysing 'La Maquina', we edge closer to capturing the football the Dutch would play to create Total Football.

What must also be noted is that, also in 1929, Ferencvaros toured South America, actually beating the Uruguay national team 3-2. The fact that they suffered defeats against São Paulo of Brazil and the Argentina national team shows how strong the game in South America already was in the late 1920s. It was an era which should have belonged to the Argentinians, but it was Uruguay who would win all the major titles.

The 'potreros' (fields) were Argentina's wasteland football pitches; similar to the grunds of Budapest or the street football youths played around the world. All football fans have seen the footage of a young Leo Messi playing on what can only be described as a wasteland, dancing around his opponents just as he would on perfect pitches as a professional. The potrero has its extra challenges, as shown on the footage as Messi has to navigate potholes and broken glass. Messi's style is the most famous of the current generation but it is a style heavily linked with the Argentinian blueprint of their number tens. It would be on the potreros that all these players would first fall in love with the game. Young kids would gather with impromptu footballs or rag balls; if someone in the neighbourhood had an actual football then this would be a luxury. Argentinian football is often criticised – but complimented at home – for its craftiness, with Maradona's 'Hand Of God' goal being the epitome of this. The art of 'picardia' (craftiness) would be born on the potreros. Carlos Peucelle was one famous product of the potreros and his transfer from Sportivo Buenos Aires to River Plate in 1931 would spark a sequence of events that led to the creation of 'La Maquina'. But, as Peucelle reminded the public on many occasions during his life, he was not solely responsible for the birth of 'La Maquina' and no one person could be credited with its creation. 'I was no one's teacher! The player is made by playing,' he once said. When Peucelle joined River Plate he would, after a year of settling in, turn back to his days on the potrero, where he was coached by a man named Félix Roldán. [16]

Peucelle was born in Buenos Aires in 1908 and died aged 81 in 1990. Often described as a winger, Peucelle was much more than that. He would often leave his starting position on the right wing and would come inside to play as a number ten or pop up on the opposite flank. His wandering style is captured in a goal scored by Argentina against Brazil in the final of the 1937 South American Championship (Americas Cup). After the game finished 0-0 and went to extra time, Argentine teenager Vincente De La Mata scored twice in the space of four minutes. The first goal summed up Peucelle's great qualities as a playmaker. Deployed on the right wing, he drifted throughout the game and, in the build-up to the first goal, was almost on the left wing when he played the ball wide for Garcia to cross for De La Mata.

Peucelle was on the books of many of Buenos Aires's clubs, but it was San Telmo where he played first-team football at the start of his career. He then transferred to Sportivo Buenos Aires, a now defunct club originally formed by a merger between Buenos Aires Isla Maciel and Sportivo Argentino. The latter was a club formed by Boca Juniors players who had a problem with the management staff of their club at the time. Sportivo managed to survive until the 1960s and this was achievable partly due to the funds that were gathered from the sale of Peucelle to River Plate in 1930 for 10,000 pesos.

Peucelle was nicknamed 'Barullo' (disorder) in a reference to the chaos he caused opponents, not through aggression but the skills he learned on the potrero. The general consensus among football observers at the time was that Peucelle had the potrero in his heart. By having this built into him, Peucelle was not only able to bring his exceptional talent to the pitch but had the ability to pick out and nurture other young players who also had the 'baldino' (vacant lot) in their footballing DNA.

Peucelle arrived at River Plate in 1931 and would go on to play for them until 1941, scoring 113 goals in 307 games. Peucelle would look towards an old friend and mentor to help guide his new club into the areas of recruitment and consultancy, with a focus on the youth players.

Félix Roldán, a newspaper salesman who had coached Peucelle as a boy, got the call from his protégé in 1932 after word got out that Roldán was unhappy with his beloved Racing Club de Avellaneda, more commonly referred to as Racing Club. The Rosario-based club had signed Evaristo Barrera, a centre-forward who blasted in 136 goals in 142 appearances. On the face of it, Barrera was a great signing but Roldán had a spirit similar to the Viennese 'Scheiberspiel'; he preferred the game to be played in a certain way and winning was not at the forefront of Roldán's football philosophy. As well as Peucelle, Roldán is credited with discovering and creating the successful careers of Bonifacio Martín and Arcadio López. In 1959, writing a paper named *The Spiral of Schemes*, Peucelle outlined his relationship with Roldán and recalled a conversation with his old friend in which

Roldán expressed his delight about a football game his team had just played: 'Yesterday the kids played. Look … I went out with my belly like this, full of soccer. What a dance, what a milonga!' When quizzed about the score, Roldán admitted his team had actually lost the game, but he was over the moon with how they played. It was this ethos that had captured Peucelle and made him force River Plate to act on Roldán's disgruntled reaction to the signing of Barrera at Racing.

Barrera was undoubtedly a fantastic goalscorer but someone who would use his brute strength to power in goals. In a slightly contradictory turn of events, River Plate would go on to sign Bernabé Ferreyra, a powerful and prolific forward who could strike a ball like no other. Ferreyra was signed in 1932 and it is unclear if Roldán had anything to do with this signing, but it seems unlikely. Ferreyra, like Peucelle, was signed for a massive transfer fee; 50,000 pesos was a world record and the first time the record had been broken by a club from outside the UK. These big-money signings earned River Plate the nickname 'Millonarios' (the Millionaires) but even clubs with money to spend need a vision like the one Roldán had for the club. His focus was on youngsters who he would scout from the youth leagues and nurture into playing the game in a style which would be the bedrock of 'La Maquina'. Roldán's policy was not about saving the club money; his interests were firmly in producing a team who played good, entertaining football.

La Masia, the academy of FC Barcelona, and the Ajax Academy are perhaps the most famous in the history of football. It was Roldán who, in the 1930s, created the blueprint for these academies. With help from Peucelle, who was still playing, Roldán was assigned the role of forming

River Plate's first academy. Peucelle would go on to say that the best thing he learned from Roldán was the importance of patience. Results, success and money will come to the players and teams who are formed and moulded over time. Roldán believed that focusing too much on immediate results would, beyond the short term, lead to failure. That he had that type of vision at a time when football was arguably still in its purest form is astounding. By pure, I mean there was little or no commercial influence and the game was simply about entertainment and the success of a team.

Today, academy bosses and club directors almost nurture talent as a way to manipulate financial fair play rules or to make profits to fund the next big superstar signing. Roldán's patience would lead to 'La Maquina' being created and becoming one of the greatest teams to ever play the game. Roldán may not be as famous as Hirschl and Peucelle, but he was certainly just as influential, if not more so. The academy that was set up would be one of the first in the world in which all the teams played in the same formation and used the same tactics – something that was hailed as revolutionary decades later when Ajax did it. Roldán was not just a person with strong beliefs around how the game should be played, he was also shrewd in developing individual players; he had a lot of input in the academy that he and Peucelle ran. Although these youth teams were not the most successful, by playing the same type of football, it allowed the players to develop better. Roldán would often tinker with players' positions, turning defenders into attackers, which is common in more recent times.

Teamed with his vision of the game, this meant that, rather than going out and buying replacements, the club would work with what they had. It helped that the players they had to work with often included the best of the crop from the surrounding teams in Argentina. River Plate would offer trials to young prospects and sign them up at a young age, allowing these players time to develop into fantastic footballers. The policy of patience Roldán instilled into the academy allowed this to happen. Adolfo Pedernera, Eduardo Correa, José Ramos, Mario Filippo and Fernando Sánchez are just some of the more famous names to emerge. Pedernera was perhaps the biggest success story of the academy. Many of these successful players joined in 1931/32 and this crop of youngsters would be nicknamed 'The Onion' by the local press. 'La Maquina' would come almost a decade later and many of these names would be at the forefront of the machinery. Once the academy was formed, attention turned to the first team again. In 1932, Imre Hirschl had arrived in Argentina. He was managing Gimnasia and he would produce a team that got everyone in the country to take notice.

Much of the evidence of Hirschl's early life is conflicting and confusing. What seems to be the most consistent account is that he was born in 1900 in Budapest and, finding himself amongst the flourishing football scene in the city, attended the university of Budapest, where he was coached and played for the first team. All this would be cited by the man himself during the height of his fame, which would come in South America many years later. Although none of it can be proved, his impact on the game in Argentina does suggest he had some sort of footballing education or exposure to the game at a decent level. There are some reports which suggest Hirschl played for Ferencváros, and Hakoah of both Vienna and New York, but there is no official evidence confirming this. What is certain is that he was working for his family's butcher business Kozma and Co. in the late 1920s. By 1928, the business began to struggle and this could be what spurred Hirschl to set his sights on a new life in South America, leaving behind his wife and son, who was only three at the time.

Hirschl arrived in Santos in September 1929 and would eventually become the coach of Gimnasia in 1932. What Hirschl had done in those three years before getting this job is unclear, although there are suggestions he met Béla Guttmann and became a trainer for Hakoah. In 1930, Hakoah New York, for whom Guttmann was now playing, arrived in South America for one of their famous tours. Guttmann has spoken of his contact with Hirschl, saying Hirschl approached him in São Paulo, begging for a job with the team and claiming to be a masseur. Guttmann hired him and he joined the tour party. Hirschl continued to work with the team as they travelled on to Argentina but he found himself left in Buenos Aires because there was not enough money to keep him. Guttmann – who, as we have already discussed, liked to tell a good tale – is also documented talking about Hirschl's coaching career. He claims that, as Hirschl was desperate to buy tickets for his family to travel from Budapest and join him in South America, he would approach clubs begging for a job as head coach and then deliberately sabotage the squad – playing a goalkeeper as a striker, for example – in a bid to get himself sacked and have the rest of his contract paid off to raise money to send back to Budapest.

According to Guttmann, this would backfire on occasions when Hirschl's teams pulled off shock results, boosting his reputation as a good coach when, in fact, he wanted the exact opposite. Although this seems far-fetched, there does appear to be some evidence of Hirschl playing bizarre line-ups when he arrived at Gimnasia, something which would end up earning him a reputation as a good trainer rather than one who was looking to be sacked as quickly as possible. Quite how Hirschl managed to get these jobs at football clubs is in dispute, as is much of his life story, but it seems he worked for the club now known as Palmeiras in Brazil before begging Guttmann for a job. This was perhaps after speaking with the then manager, his fellow countryman Jeno Medgyessy, in the same manner that he approached Guttmann.

Medgyessy was then dismissed after a run of bad results and Hirschl took over the club for a number of games. However, when Medgyessy was re-hired in 1930, Hirschl found himself out of a job. This is around the time that he managed to get on board with Hakoah in a trainer-physio role.

There is no documentary evidence that he ever played an official game for Hakoah or that he had any input in their tactical set-up and, when he was left behind in Buenos Aires by Hakoah, it seems that life was a struggle for Hirschl, who had still not been able to raise the funds to have his wife and child join him in South America. According to a feature about Hirschl published in the Argentinian newspaper *Nemzeti Sport* in 1932, he was living at a refuge and used his spare time to learn Spanish in a bid to become a football coach. After this uncertain period comes some light, as Hirschl took charge of Gimnasia in 1932 after again seemingly begging for them to give him a chance. Gimnasia, champions in 1929, were now struggling and they reluctantly turned to the confident Hungarian, who could no speak Spanish.

The Argentinian league was now professional and Hirschl was the first foreigner to be hired in such a role at a professional club. Guttmann claims that, during his first few weeks as manager, Hirschl was again desperate to get himself sacked for financial reasons. This seems almost plausible given that the first moves Hirschl made were to drop a number of the best players and opt for untested youth players. He took over in mid-season and Gimnasia recorded only three wins in his first 16 games. However, they managed a decent enough seventh-place finish at the end of that season.

* * *

The start of the 1933 season could not have got off to a better start for Hirschl (unless he *was* trying to get himself sacked) as his side recorded five straight victories and led the league at the midway point of the season. This sent ripples across the country, as the focus was mainly on the so-called big clubs. Now, everyone was taking notice of Gimnasia, asking how a team who usually found themselves in mid-table were topping the league. Hirschl was getting the recognition. He was a good public speaker – a trait many of the trainers and coaches we have discussed seemed to have – and spoke of how the first few months of his time at Gimnasia were tough because the players were unprofessional and needed a lot of discipline and guidance to unlock their potential. Hirschl would often perform bar crawls on the hunt for his players, sending them home before they got too intoxicated. He brought in strict new training methods which included introducing basketball, sprints, long runs and gymnastics.

A number of their famous wins against the biggest sides in Argentina were achieved by the Gimnasia players

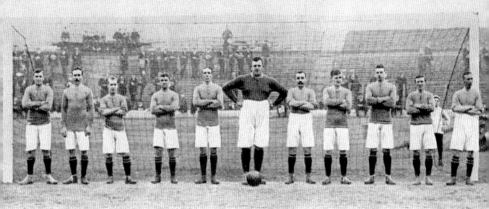

Chelsea team photo from 1905 with the great John Tait Robertson fourth from right and goalkeeper William 'Fatty' Foulke in the middle.

Gyula Mándi (date unknown), one of the great players of MTK and future coach who helped spread the work of Hogan and Robertson.

MTK Budapest in 1920 as they played FC Bayern Munich and won 7-1.

Jimmy Hogan in 1946 on his coaching tour whilst back in England after taking it around the world first.

Hugo Meisl, one of the most influential people in taking the game of football to the next level and around the world.

Austria v Italy in the semi-final of the 1934 World Cup. Italian forward Enrique Guaita is captured here scoring the only goal of the game.

Matthias Sindelar outside of his coffee house after his retirement from football.

The core of River Plate's 'La Máquina' from left to right; Juan C. Muñoz, José M. Moreno, Adolfo Pedernera, Angel Labruna and Félix Lousteau in 1941.

England v Hungary 1953. Ferenc Puskas leads out the golden team with Billy Wright of England leading out his side in the match of the century.

A mural found in Budapest celebrating the great win over the English in 1953.

A young Rinus Michels in a game played in London in 1954.

Ajax trainer Jack Reynolds, the man who laid some of the foundations for the modern Ajax. He is pictured speaking at a party accompanied by his wife

Michels training his players ahead of a clash with Feyenoord in 1966 and the creation of Total Football.

Vic Buckingham, the godfather of Total Football keeping his eye on a training session while Fulham manager in 1967.

Ajax team of 1971. Back row, left to right: Barry Hulshoff, Heinz Stuy, Wim Suurbier, Dick van Dijk, Gerrie Muhren. Front row, left to right: Piet Keizer, Sjaak Swart, Piet Rijnders, Velibor Vasovic, Johan Cruyff, Johan Neeskens

A young Johan Cruyff in 1965 – arguably not only the greatest player but the greatest coach and greatest mind in football history.

physically outlasting their opponents rather than blowing them away with a new brand of football. But Hirschl did bring some Hungarian influence to the team's style of play. Bizarrely, the Hungarian style was seen as being more direct than that of the Argentinian game at the time and Hirschl used to take advantage of the long ball when needed, stating that he did not have much time for his forwards entertaining with the ball and would prefer for them to play forward passes. However, he allowed his team to play with freedom going forward. They went on to finish fifth (joint fourth with River Plate) after an extremely controversial end to the season which saw Gimnasia on the receiving end of some dubious refereeing decisions. This started in a game against Boca on Christmas Eve when Gimnasia took a 2-0 lead but, after some shocking decisions by referee De Dominicis, they lost 3-2. De Dominicis was suspended by the league for his performance and alleged bias in that game.

A couple of weeks later, when trailing 2-1 against San Lorenzo, what appeared to be a clear penalty for Gimnasia was instead given as a free kick outside the area. Things got even worse when a tame shot on goal was easily saved by the Gimnasia keeper but a goal was inexplicably awarded, the referee deeming the ball had crossed the goal line. With Gimnasia feeling helpless in the face of this officiating, the players staged an on-pitch protest, sitting on the floor and allowing San Lorenzo to score goal after goal. When the score reached 7-1, the game was abandoned. The protest was supported by coach Hirschl, whose hard work could not get past old-fashioned bias or cheating. Following these controversies, Gimnasia went on to lose a number of other games towards the end of the season, but they still finished as the highest scorers (90), although they also conceded the most goals (55) among the top seven teams. His early work at Gimnasia, which included replacing some of the established stars with youth players, shows that he was clearly an excellent coach with an eye for the type of players he needed to make his teams successful.

It wasn't just tactically and physically that Hirschl impacted Gimnasia. He introduced a rule that all the players would be paid the same salary to, as he put it, ensure a common level of sacrifice. He also promoted a number of players from the youth team, deciding to stay away from making new signings at a time when the bigger clubs were all making big signings for big fees. Hirschl preferred to develop and train the players he had at his disposal. Among them was Arturo Naón, who would go on to become their main goalscorer and was a fantastic talent. There was also José María Minella, who started out as a forward but was switched to centre-half and would start many of the attacks Naón ended up finishing.

Hirschl's side would earn the nickname 'El Expreso Platense', which reflected the team's ability to demolish every team in front of them, including the big clubs. This great attacking football would get Hirschl recognised countrywide and would convince River Plate to hire him in 1935. He arrived at the club at a time when they were just about to see their academy products ripen into some of the best players to represent the club. Gimnasia had broken into the top five teams in Argentina and this had upset those at the top; a conspiracy theory backed up by quite a lot of facts is that Gimnasia probably would have gone on to win the championship had it not been for some biased refereeing. Hirschl perhaps recognised that, with a club such as Gimnasia, you could only go as far as nearly toppling the powers at the top of the Argentinian footballing hierarchy and the best solution was to join them.

Much about Hirschl's life story has been disputed and contested, but it is clear he was a character who had a love for the game of football. Perhaps it was luck that his Gimnasia side took so well to his changes, but many successes in football could be classed as luck and the commitment Hirschl had to making Gimnasia successful appears to contradict Guttmann's claims that he was using football to secure a quick payout to bring family to South America. His family did join him shortly after he took the job at Gimnasia, only to return to Europe soon afterwards due to homesickness. Hirschl would remain in South America for the rest of his life, remarrying and having more children.

When Hirschl arrived at River Plate, the academy Roldán had founded was bubbling away and Peucelle and Ferreyra were playing at the top of their games. Hirschl would be the man tasked with making sure the club fulfilled its potential. This was not the blank canvas he had at Gimnasia; this was the richest team in Argentina and could have provided the perfect payout had he not succeeded, but succeed he did. The River Plate academy was now a number of years old since Roldán had been in charge of it. The young talents in the academy were often poached from the lesser teams in Argentina; a similar story to what happens at Ajax, Barcelona and most of the clubs competing at the top of the modern game.

Sir Alex Fergusons 'Class of 92' were made up of the best talent the clubs in Manchester and the surrounding area had to offer and it was no different in the 1930s, although compensation may have been a lot less lucrative back then when the bigger clubs came calling for young talent. It is sometimes suggested that what Hirschl created at Gimnasia was the first draft of 'La Maquina' but, other than the coach, I do not believe there is enough to link the two together. This is a view supported by Argentinian football historian Esteban Bekerman, who offered his priceless knowledge when researching this era.

Hirschl took charge of River Plate for the 1935/36 season and was their first foreign coach and also the first coach River Plate paid another club money for. Hirschl was joined at the club by one of his best players at Gimnasia, centre-half Minella. River Plate finished fifth in his first season but what was most important about this campaign was that Hirschl promoted a number of players from the academy into the first team. Some of these would write their names in the history books as part of the machine that was being slowly built, serviced and finely tuned, a machine that would go on to influence modern football, not only in South America but across the world, just as the teams of the 'Danubian School' had done in earlier decades. It is highly likely that, when Hirschl was learning the game, he attended one of the many lectures Jimmy Hogan gave in Budapest. This knowledge, combined with Roldán and Peucelle's eye for young talent, was a perfect mix.

* * *

José Manuel Moreno, Adolfo Alfredo Pedernera, Aristóbulo Luis Deambrossi and Aarón Wergifker, all still teenagers at the time, were the first products who were born from Roldán's academy of 1932. They were perhaps the most influential of the debutants in those early seasons that Hirschl was at River Plate and their inclusion soon rewarded the manager and the club with much-needed success. In 1936, River Plate secured the league title by winning 13 of their 17 league games. Scoring the most goals (49) and conceding the least goals[19], it was a dominant conquering of the Argentinian top division. Playing a similar style to the one Hirschl introduced to Gimnasia and with a higher calibre of player (plus no refereeing bias), River Plate were unstoppable. The following season, the league format changed meaning all 18 clubs would play each other twice, in previous seasons teams only played each other once over the course of the season. The club again won the title, more than doubling the amount of goals they scored.Independiente actually equalled their astonishing 106-goal haul and it must be noted that most teams also doubled the amount of goals they had scored the previous season.

River Plate's youngsters were now starting to show that their ceiling as players was nowhere near being reached and that they were only going to get better and better. Two titles had been won with a mix of the big-money signings from 'The Millionaires' team and youngsters from the academy and youth leagues. The youngsters who had came in had exceeded even the expectations of Peucelle and what was great about this team was that things were only going to get better. In 1938, however, Independiente did break River Plate's stranglehold on the title, finishing two points ahead of them and Hirschl left at the end of the season to return to Gimnasia. How would River Plate replace him and continue their progress? This was a question Roldán and Peucelle most likely already knew the answer to.

Renato Cesarini was born in Italy but, only a few months after his birth, his family packed up and moved to Buenos Aires. Cesarini became a footballer in Argentina, playing for a number of clubs there, but he never broke into the top five clubs and was bought by Juventus, moving back to Italy. He was a midfielder or striker who was remembered for scoring late, decisive goals. He played in the European competitions Hugo Meisl had created and represented the Italian national team in the early 1930s.

When Hirschl needed to boost his River Plate team's title bid in 1936, 30-year-old Cesarini was signed, not only for his goalscoring and game-deciding reputation but also because he was a disciple of the 'Danubian School'. When Hirschl left, it created an opportunity for Cesarini to take the reins with the help of Víctor Caamaño, who had won the league with River Plate in 1932. Cesarini had all the pieces to the machine but would he read and understand the manual and assemble it correctly? The 1939 season would end the same way as the previous one, with River Plate finishing second to Independiente, this time by six points. However, it was becoming more apparent just how deadly this team would become; they were renowned for hammering teams and their resounding victories included one 8-0 scoreline. José Manuel Moreno was now reaching the peak of his powers. He was a player similar to Diego Maradona – on and off the pitch. He believed the best way to train was by dancing the tango and he was often out into the early hours at the tango hall, surrounded by beautiful women. When critics condemned his social life, he didn't care, stating that it never affected his performances on the pitch and that he had never missed a training session.

With ten games left in the 1939 season and with Independiente playing consistently, River Plate couldn't afford to slip up against them when they played each other. River Plate lost 3-2 and Moreno was punished for his lack of discipline. The player defended himself, insisting that, on the eve of this game, it was the only time in his career that he had gone to bed early. His team-mates backed him up, going on strike for the remaining nine games of the season.

This was an opportunity for a number of the academy players to be thrown in. Ángel Labruna would be one of those youth players who got the nod and he took full advantage, cementing his place in the team and becoming another key part of the machine that was being constructed. Labruna would go on to become River Plate's record goalscorer, netting 317 times in official matches across the 20-year period he played for them. In 1939, Hirschl was now Rosario Central manager and he was on the end of a thrashing when his team faced River Plate that season. Following Rosario's 6-0 defeat, he suggested he had suffered the result of his own teachings, stating: 'Those six goals were scored by my boys.' That is quite a claim and something Peucelle would constantly dismiss. Peucelle believed there were multiple factors which influenced good football and he always insisted that no one manager created 'La Maquina'. He felt it was a peer-influenced affair rather than a single coach's bright idea, a view supported by the success of the academy and what happened to the team in the years before 1941.

The 1940 season saw River Plate finish only third despite boasting the most goals scored and this campaign could have been seen as the beginning of the end for this great side, but 'La Maquina' had not even been born yet. Roldán had not yet completed the blueprint. Félix Loustau was signed from Buenos Aires-based Dock Sud to play in the youth team and Roldán had a plan for the left-footed defender. He converted him into a left-winger and received positive reviews from Peucelle when he asked him for his feedback on the player's performances. Loustau would repay his mentors by becoming part of the club's greatest team. Another signing from Dock

Sud, made in 1939 on Roldán's recommendation, was Juan Carlos Muñoz. He would eventually become the fifth and final part of River Plate's classic attacking quintet when he broke into the team in 1941, the year 'La Maquina' were officially born. As the 1941 season got off to a bad start, Peucelle began to have more and more of an impact on the minds of the players and manager Cesarini. Peucelle was still a player at the beginning of this season but was spending more of his time working on the next generation.

He was injecting his knowledge of the passing game and his ability to read and understand where to find space on the pitch into his team-mates and the youth players he helped nurture. Both of these concepts (the passing game and mobility around the pitch) derived from the 'Danubian School'. Sadly, just as all of Felix Roldán's hard work was about to fully click together with the firing of the engines of 'La Maquina', Roldán passed away. The mantle was now fully passed on to Peucelle and his input came just in time.

Cesarini seemed to be getting a number of things wrong in the 1941 campaign. Pedernera's talent was clear but, despite recommendations from Peucelle and everyone else who had seen him play, Cesarini was not convinced and started the season with Rivero as centre-forward, replacing him with D'Alessandro. Pedernera was chopped and changed around the pitch for the needs of the team rather than cementing a fixed position and was eventually dropped completely. River Plate only accumulated 11 points from nine games and finally, as they were gearing up to face Independiente, Cesarini gave in to the pressure and started Pedernera at centre-forward.

Peucelle is believed to have told Cesarini that Pedernera must be used at centre-forward because he played for the team and would bring those around him into the game; with D'Alessandro at centre-forward, the team had to play for him to get the best out of him. The role Pedernera played for River Plate was another early prototype of the 'false nine' Pep Guardiola would make famous and of the withdrawn centre-forward role which had been seen in Hungary and Poland and even in England where G.O. Smith of Corinthians was the very first to play this way. River Plate beat Independiente 2-1 with a goal from Pedernera and, with Peucelle, Moreno, Labruna and Deambrossi all playing, the famous attacking line was starting to take shape. However, Cesarini was still not convinced and D'Alessandro won back his place ahead of Pedernera, who would return to playing in a number of positions before again finding himself out of the starting XI. That was until River Plate faced Independiente again and Peucelle demanded Cesarini use Pedernera at centre-forward.

The coach gave in, River Plate scored a famous 4-0 win with a hat-trick from Pedernera and 'La Maquina' was born. River Plate followed that with a 4-0 victory over Lanús and, on 19 October 1941, they crushed reigning champions Boca Juniors 5-1. This was the penultimate game of the season and River Plate needed a win to secure the title. Although the nickname 'La Maquina' would not be coined until 1942, José Gabriel wrote in *Diario Crítica* after the victory over Boca: 'They looked like a little machine.'

Boca had been torn apart and Peucelle's influence on the creation of 'La Maquina' cannot be disputed. He was now retired, but his influence was not only injected into the players, his ethos and feelings around the game of football connected River Plate to its fans more than ever before. Yes, they were playing to win games, but there was also a sense that they knew they had a responsibility to entertain the fans with their style of play; a South American 'Scheiberspiel'. The reshaped River Plate's surge in the latter stages of the season secured the title despite a poor start to the campaign and this was just a glimpse of the levels to which Roldán's youth academy would take the team.

Peucelle did not want to take all the credit for the products of the great academy and wrote an open letter to the fans in 1945 in which he stated that the best players in the team were products of the youth set-up and were all 'encouraged by professional players who transmitted their teachings; they had a vision of what the contribution of these teams would mean over the years, if they knew how to conduct them with intelligence and above all with patience. The period of selection until consecration lasts five years (14–19 years). This work is carried out with all efficiency by people who generally remain anonymous.'

These 'anonymous' people were the coaches of the youth teams, who were never paid for their work; people who did it for the love of the game, and the club would be forever in debt to these volunteers who helped shape the club's success in the 1940s. During the first season of 'La Maquina' (1941), the starting XI included seven players from the academy. The number would only increase over the next few seasons.

The 1942 season would see Loustau feature more prominently as the forward quintet became famous (Muñóz, Moreno, Pedernera, Labruna and Loustau). Although they would only play together for the first team 18 times in five years, they became the stars of the side. Loustau's introduction was believed to be down to Deambrossi after he recommended to Peucelle that Loustau had been waiting long enough without much game time and deserved a chance.

Loustau took that chance and repaid Deambrossi by taking his place, the latter rarely featuring again.

The nickname 'La Maquina' was first attached to the team after a 6-2 win over Chacarita in June 1942. The River Plate style of football was a dynamic one during the 'La Maquina' era. The 3-2-2-3 (W-M) formation was slightly adapted into almost a 3-2-5. Centre-forward Pedernera would drop deeper, allowing space for the wide men, Loustau on the left and Muñóz on the right, who were integral to the system, supporting both the attack and defence. With Pedernera dropping back, Labruna and Moreno would exploit the areas traditionally occupied by a centre-forward. Labruna was the chief goalscorer, ruthless and a brute whenever he got a glimpse of the goal. Moreno would often drift even deeper than Pedernera and launch attacks, sometimes from deep in his own half.

The result was a style often described as football being played by artists, an orchestra. The five forwards did not stay fixed to their positions and would intertwine and move freely. Boasting fantastic skill and understanding but also physical stamina, the academy had built them for this. The legendary status of the 'La Maquina' team is sometimes questioned because the players regarded as the stars only played together 18 times. Peucelle always maintained that the success of the team was not just the famous forward line but the harmony between the whole side. Every player played their part and they produced some amazing performances in the years 1941–47, which is the timescale generally given to the lifespan of this team. Opinions differ as to who was the best player or star of the team. Moreno's discipline had been seen as a problem by Hirschl, but the fact he was still a crucial part of the squad shows just how much talent he had. Loustau once recalled how, with the team about to play against Racing Club, Moreno had been admitted to hospital the evening before suffering from alcohol intoxication; he was told if he played, even for 20 minutes, he could die. Moreno discharged himself from hospital, played the whole 90 minutes and was the best player on the pitch.

He was a real entertainer and had the personality to match his football. The forward line was backed up by a stubborn defence and the team had an aura about them that they could shut off a game when they wanted to. They would also dedicate some time in each game to showing off daft skills and executing complicated combinations with the ball to repay the fans who had come to watch them. Every player was an attacker and every player defended and the team won the ball high up the pitch whenever they could. Defenders would join in with attacks and, with the whole team working in harmony, players would move around the pitch to fit the needs of the team.

They are a team revered even by people who never saw them play live. Much like the Dutch of the 1970s and the Hungarians of the 1950s, many of these feelings are perhaps more romantic than reality, but there is no doubt 'La Maquina' played a brand and style of football that follows the textbook of the great teams previously discussed. They were an exceptional team but not invincible, perhaps not reaching the dominance in terms of trophies that their football deserved. They won the title in 1942 and 1945 but lost out to Boca in 1943 and 1944. River Plate reclaimed the title in 1947, but a young Alfredo Di Stéfano had replaced the departing Pedernera by this point, so that title is often not included in the 'La Maquina' era.

The team's failure to totally monopolise the Argentinian title returns us to the suggestion that playing such a style of football is not successful. But what *is* success?

A team that will be remembered forever for the way they played is success, surely? Muñóz perhaps explained why the team did not always deliver the results expected when he was once quoted as saying: 'We went out on the pitch and played our way; take the ball, give it to me, a gambit, this, that and the goal came by itself. Generally it took a long time for the goal to come and the anguish was because games were not settled quickly. Inside the box, of course, we wanted to score, but in the midfield we had fun. There was no rush. It was instinctive.' This approach was no doubt bred in the youth academy, was built into the players. It was the Harley 'short to foot' style mixed with Argentinian flair and desire, developed under Hirschl's coaching and guidance and then by Peucelle passing down his experience. 'La Maquina' changed the landscape of the game of football forever. Di Stéfano was asked later in his career who the top five footballers in the history of the game were; his reply was Muñóz, Moreno, Pedernera, Labruna and Loustau.

The five marvellous forwards of 'La Maquina' tick a lot of boxes when looking at the culture and background of Total Football. Pedernera was not only influential on the pitch, he helped set up the first players' union in Argentina, ensuring that players were rewarded suitably now that the game was professional. Labruna, who scored 293 goals in 515 appearances, remains the leading goalscorer in Argentine football. He tried to leave the game behind when he retired but, after failing in a number of business ventures including a pizzeria, a car dealership and a hotel, he knew he had to return to football.

After playing for River Plate virtually his whole career, it was fitting that he should return as manager, winning a further six trophies as he brought an end to a long drought for the club. Labruna would go on to be a successful manager at a number of clubs.

When examining managers linked to Total Football and similar styles of play and what made them successful, there always seems to be a sense that they put the interests of their team and the game as a whole ahead of their own. All managers strive to be successful, of course, but a trait Hirschl had was that, whatever he wanted to achieve or gain from football, he made sure the clubs he managed reaped the biggest benefits. At every club Hirschl worked at before and after River Plate, his success was built around fringe or youth players. He would train and coach these players until they reached a high level and, although Hirschl would move on to another club, he would leave behind a club primed for a period of success that may never have happened without his influence. The young players he promoted were no doubt born with great talent and Hirschl was not a miracle worker who created superstars from scratch, but he did have a talent for spotting potential. Although he coached players to play in a free and entertaining way, the key lesson he taught his players was to play with efficiency.

The Dutch team of the 1970s were extremely efficient in the sense that the reason players switched positions and played with the freedom they did was to be more efficient with the ball and the space available to them. You can watch a game today and the data collected will pick out the player who has run furthest or covered the most ground, but the data will also show who has been the most efficient with and without the ball, who has played the most key passes, who has made the most forward runs. Hirschl had none of this data; he had to work with his beliefs, knowledge and experience in the game. It is clear that he was a well-educated football thinker. Peucelle seems to embody the football culture captured throughout our story, a player-turned-coach whose vision and expertise helped shape 'La Maquina'. Peucelle went on to comment about the game in published articles and books. He often said that he did not like to give labels to different styles of football. He argued: 'No one invented "La Maquina". It existed because there were circumstances at the same time and in the same club.' Following the 1945 title win, Peucelle wrote in the club magazine that the success was owed in full to the club investing in youth and the delicate task of discovering, perfecting and forming future stars. This was a homage to his great friend Félix Roldán. Peucelle would often dismiss his own role in the development of the team, stating that he was never anyone's teacher, as it is the player that plays.

Roldán's River Plate academy may not be as famous as La Masia or the Ajax Academy but, just as those systems would later do, it produced one of the greatest teams ever. What gave Roldán this great idea? And how did he know the type of player who could be moulded into a star? In modern-day football, there are countless established coaching methods and guidance on how to coach players at all levels is widely available. Back then, it would all have been a direct result of people watching the game live and coming up with new ideas. However, by the 1940s, as communications improved, it was becoming easier to spread the word about football methods, which is why the net begins to bring in a larger haul when looking at the years leading up to the Dutch of the 1970s. Coaches and managers wanted to play like the 'Wunderteam' and 'La Maquina'. Just as it was after the innovations of the Hungarians and then the Austrians, football was a different game altogether after 'La Maquina'. But how did this new football style end up in Europe? How did it make its way to the Netherlands and why did it take 30 years to do so?

The birth of the W-M tinkering

At the same time as 'La Maquina' was operating, Ernő Egri Erbstein was building his career as a coach. He had spent the 1930s perfecting his skills at a number of clubs in Italy, only for his progress to be sabotaged by the Second World War. Despite facing a ban from working due to his Jewish heritage, his influence at Torino help create one of the greatest teams in Italy's history, a team tragically cut off in its prime by the Superga air disaster on 4 May 1949. Dominic Bliss captured Erbstein's life in his book *The Triumph and Tragedy of Football's Forgotten Pioneer*. Erbstein was born in 1898 in Oradea (Nagyvárad), which was part of the Austro-Hungarian Empire at the time. He was part of the footballing scene in Budapest and played for BAK, remaining on their books for around seven years. Erbstein then moved to Italy where he played for a number of clubs before becoming a manager. Erbstein, drawing on his Hungarian football roots, helped Bari win many admirers in Italian football in the late 1920s with their expressive, attacking football. It did not bring success, though.

The team were relegated in 1929 and Erbstein's contract ended. Following spells at Nocerina and Cagliari and a return to Bari, Erbstein ended up in the city of Lucca in Tuscany when he became coach of Lucchese. It was in Lucca that Erbstein would establish himself as a great footballing thinker. We know that 'La Maquina' was built on shrewd scouting and a keen eye for a great player. Throughout his career as a trainer or manager, Erbstein would also unearth some fantastic talents. Benito Mussolini's influence loomed large over football. Countless promising players would see their careers halted, stalled or even ended for their anti-fascist beliefs.

The FIGC (Italian football's governing body) was an arm of the Fascist Sports Ministry at the time and had the final say on all managerial or player registrations. What Erbstein was brave enough to do was give these exiled footballers a team to play for and continue their development. It no doubt put him on the radar of the fascist authorities but during his time at Lucchese he was able to use this tactic to bring him the first major successes of his coaching career. During his five seasons with Lucchese, he took them from Serie C to Serie A, their promotion to the top flight secured with a fantastic title-winning season in 1935/36. This led to interest from bigger clubs and Erbstein was also being driven away from Lucca by the fact it had become a fascist stronghold. Although he was wanted by Lazio, he perhaps considered that being a foreign Jew in Rome was a risk not worth taking, so he headed for the liberal city of Turin in 1938. Erbstein was afforded a hefty budget to build his side at Torino, but instead of signing big-name stars he opted to put his faith in the club's youngsters and to buy players he knew from his successful time in the lower divisions.

Torino had a new young president who loved the game of football. Ferruccio Novo was a full-back in his youth career for Torino but never quite made the grade. He would prove integral to Erbstein's success, backing the brand of football the coach wished to introduce. Novo had actually discussed in board meetings the importance of Torino implementing a set style of play and it would seem this was now becoming just as important to club directors as working out ways to bring more fans to the ground or clinching a new signing. At this time, England was still where managers and directors looked for inspiration, particularly after what Herbert Chapman had done with Arsenal. Erbstein was brought in not just to win matches but to instil a modern style of play, introduce new training techniques and, most importantly, lay down a method of working that was to be filtered throughout the club, just as Roldán had done in Argentina.

* * *

In the story of Total Football's evolution, certain individuals are as important as teams. One such character is Raffaele Vallone, one of the players Erbstein plucked from the youth ranks of Italian football. Although not one of Erbstein's greatest players, Vallone's story is fascinating and captures many of the elements that would cuff themselves to the Total Football brand during a time when fascism was tearing apart the world and impacting Jewish communities across the globe.

Vallone wasn't just a football man, he was much more. Hollywood and Italians have always been a good mix. I mean, how many Italian gangster movies can there be? But when sportsmen and women dabble in the movie world, it is often quite disastrous, especially for footballers. I do apologise to any Vinnie Jones fans, as he has made a decent enough career from it. 'Raf', as Vallone was best known, was not only a capable enough footballer to be part of one of Italy's greatest-ever club sides, he was also a lawyer, a journalist and, most successfully, an actor who conquered not only Italian cinema but broke into Hollywood.

Vallone was born in 1916 in Tropea, Calabria, on the western coast of the region which occupies the toe of the Italian boot. It is a beautiful, picturesque location often credited with being one of the country's hidden gems. Hidden, as in this area is often looked down upon by outsiders and more so by Italians in the north as being crime-ridden and corrupt. A very unfair prejudice was and still is cast over the southern part of the country. I can only guess this was the reason Vallone's father, an ambitious young lawyer, decided to move the family north to Turin in 1918 and set up his own legal practice. Vallone grew up under the guidance of his father, who made sure he stayed on the right path. Vallone fell in love with football and, at 14, Torino considered taking him on. His powerful, athletic physique and footballing ability had caught the eye of the professional club. His dad wasn't so keen on letting his son throw away the promise of a career in the family business and only allowed his son to join the club on the condition that he would divide his attention equally between his studies and his football. His father's reservations were not to do with money; compared to the average working man, Vallone would have been making considerably more as a professional footballer.

Vallone managed to successfully juggle his football and studies. After graduating from high school, he enrolled at Turin University, where he studied philosophy and law. He made his first-team debut for Torino in 1934. In this maiden season with the first team, Vallone picked up his first winner's medal when Torino won the Coppa Italia. Still only a teenager, Raf was only used a handful of times that season, possibly partly as a result of him focusing on his studies. His lack of appearances would be a common feature and he barely made it into double figures in his first four years as a Torino player. To his father's delight, he successfully graduated and Torino still had a place for him, as his bullish physique suited their forward line whenever they called upon him. Vallone, though, was far from a regular but perhaps he needed a manager who would show faith in him. Then along came perhaps Torino's greatest-ever coach and a period in which the club would climb the footballing ranks and become one of Europe's most dominant sides.

The great Erbstein – who not only revolutionised the game but escaped labour camps in the process of doing so – was the perfect man to help nurture the intelligent Vallone. As the squad took shape under Erbstein, Raf took his place in the Torino midfield more regularly than in his previous seasons. He made 15 appearances and scored three goals in the 1938/39 season. Erbstein brought a somewhat educational feel to his style of coaching. This included a pre-match session of an hour or so in which he would outline tactics on a blackboard. The players are said to have called this the 'Killer Hour' but, to Vallone, it felt like part of his usual routine, with him being so used to sitting in lecture halls and studying.

Erbstein's training sessions were intense and could also be summed up as a 'killer' in some ways. They were based around the theory of learning through fun via various games, which would end up being highly competitive. Most importantly, Erbstein passed on his football knowledge, taken from the Hungarian football of the early 1900s, the Scottish passing style and Herbert Chapman's explosive counter-attacking game. Erbstein was a fantastic man-manager and this is perhaps why he did not always need household names in his teams to achieve success. He also believed happiness bred success, offering this fascinating insight: 'Smile in the changing room and when you go out on to the pitch. If the opposition goes in hard or the referee is wrong, smile. If he is wrong again, smile. If the opposition scores, smile. If we score, smile, smile, smile! If the opposition insults us, offends us, smile!'

In Dominic Bliss's book on Erbstein, he uses quotes from Vallone which recalled his feelings while playing under Erbstein at Torino and how watching Rinus Michels's Ajax and Netherlands teams reminded him of the side he played in. 'As long ago as that, Erbstein exploited the wide areas, making use of every corner of the pitch. We were playing some sort of Total Football. Every time one of us had the ball, his team-mates were on the move in order to give him not one but three different options.' This supports the idea that Chapman was a huge influence on Erbstein, as the approach Vallone describes almost mirrors the adaptations Chapman made to create his successful Arsenal side, using the space as an ally to exploit and launch attacks into. Erbstein wanted his side to become a hard-pressing unit when they did not have the ball and a free-flowing, risk-taking team when attacking. Sadly, the relationship between Vallone and Erbstein was cut short.

On 3 December 1938, Erbstein had to leave his position as manager when Mussolini followed the example set by the Nazis by bringing in anti-Semitic laws. Erbstein left with Torino joint top of Serie A after starting the season with six wins, two draws and only one defeat. Vallone, by this point, had fallen fully for football, thanks to Erbstein and his philosophy. Although Erbstein continued to influence the team in an unofficial role as an adviser, it was not until after the war that he was able to make an official return. It was then, of course, that he helped to create the 'Grande Torino' side that conquered Italy for eight years, winning five consecutive scudetti before the Superga air disaster in 1949 killed all 31 passengers on the plane including all the players, Erbstein and his coaching staff, journalists and crew.

Raf Vallone was not on the fateful flight as, by then, he had left behind the game he adored, his football dreams ruined in 1941 by the dark side of Italian football and culture. Explaining his decision to turn his back on football, Vallone said: 'Do you know why I retired from football? I played in the national team ... in Vienna and I discovered that the match was tricked [fixed] for political reasons. I was very disappointed and I decided to give up. The trick in Vienna was one [of] the biggest disappointments of my life.'

Vallone quit and joined the family law firm. A man of honesty, the injustice of the fixed match did not sit right with him and, during his time with the law firm, he became increasingly agitated with the state of world current affairs, most notably Mussolini's dictatorship and the increasing threat of Nazi Germany. Vallone joined the staff at the left-wing newspaper *L'Unità* and his sharp observations and superbly written articles saw him rise through the ranks at a rapid pace, becoming the newspaper's head of culture.

Alongside his work at *L'Unità*, Raf established himself as a drama and film critic for *La Stampa*, the daily newspaper in Turin. It was this role which opened the final door in his wonderful career path, a door that Vallone would go through and not come back out of. He was about to become a world famous actor. The 'neorealist' genre was growing at the time in Italy and would be the base for Vallone's acting career. Film budgets were relatively low and there was a trend for 'real people' to be cast in movies rather than established film stars. Directors were looking at everyone they met as a potential actor who might feature in their next movie.

Vallone made his first appearance on the big screen in 1942 when he played a sailor – a role which was not much more than that of an extra – in Goffredo Alessandrini's *Noi Vivi* (We the Living). His big break would come in 1949. Film director Giuseppe De Santis was working on his latest movie, *Bitter Rice*, a story centred around a woman working in the rice fields of the Po Valley, and decided Vallone's physical stature and rough, chiselled features would make him the perfect big-screen 'hunk'. *Bitter Rice* became a box office smash and is recognised as one the best movies made during the successful 'neorealist' era. While the majority of the 'real life' people asked to become actors overnight were discarded after one film, Vallone would go on to become a star.

He featured in many of De Santis's movies, including *No Peace Under the Olive Tree* (1950) and *Rome 11am* (1952). In the 1950s, he was a busy man, featuring in 29 films. Curzio Malaparte, mainly known for his literature, directed *The Forbidden Christ* (1951) in which Raf Vallone played the lead role of Bruno. Curzio described Vallone as 'the only Marxist face of Italian cinema', a compliment Raf appreciated. In 1950, on the set of *The Walk of Hope*, Vallone would meet his future wife, Elena Varzi, for the first time. They went on to marry and have three children. It is also believed that Vallone had a relationship with the famous French actress Brigitte Bardot towards the end of the 1950s, but he stayed married to Varzi for 50 years.

As the 'neorealist' genre fell out of favour in Italy, Vallone turned his attention to the stage, travelling to Paris and London before landing a role in *A View from the Bridge* by Peter Brook, an adaptation of Arthur Miller's play. Vallone played the role of Eddie Carbone for 550 nights at the Theatre Antoine, Paris, where he frequently received a standing ovation. This performance would earn him his chance to hit the big screens again when, in 1961, Sidney Lumet made a film version of the play. Vallone played the same part as he had on stage and the film was shot in both French and English. He had made it to Hollywood.

Towards the end of his career, he only really made cameo appearances, most notably alongside Michael Caine in *The Italian Job* (1969) and with Al Pacino in *The Godfather Part III* (1990). From Total Football to the box office; Vallone is evidence of just how strong the culture behind football is. Often players are harshly branded as 'dumb' and accused of being socially disconnected from the real world. Recently, Marcus Rashford disproved this with his campaign over free school meals, showing he was more capable of relating to real life than those in power. The same can be said of Vallone with his work in journalism and the way he hung up his boots when he saw the dark side of football. Vallone walked away from the game he loved but was fortunate to have the talent to make a good career away from it. As fans, we can take on board what he did and remember to stand up for the principles behind our love for the game. This is particularly relevant in the current era of high profile takeovers of some of football's best-known clubs and concerns over state ownership.

While Vallone turned his back on football, the great Erbstein secured his legacy with 'Grande Torino', a team who took another step closer to the Total Football style created by the Dutch. Elsewhere, Hungarians who had sat in those football lessons from Hogan in Budapest were now retiring from playing and becoming managers and coaches with some of the biggest clubs and national teams around Europe. As the conflict across Europe began to slow down, many would return home. Would this allow Hungary itself to benefit from its own creation?

Part 4

Back to Hungary

AS THE Second World War ripped through Europe and destroyed so many lives, for many in Hungary the only way to survive was to get out of the country and continue to try to make a living. Many of those involved in football had to flee across the borders to neighbouring countries or to South America.

Márton Bukovi was a centre-half who played for Ferencváros and when he had to retire early due to injury, he compared it to an opera singer losing their voice. His influence on Hungarian football would not be over, though, as he became a coach. In 1935, he had entered Yugoslavia and was staying in Zagreb when he became the coach of Građanski and implemented a tactical adjustment to his forward line, asking them to drop back into midfield. It was a tactic which proved rewarding for River Plate, but what it would bring the Hungarian national team in the 1950s would arguably top that success. An horrific leg break suffered in 1930 would eventually lead to Bukovi's retirement, but he was able to recover sufficiently to play for a few years more, moving to France in 1933 to play for Sète before retiring in 1934. During his time in Sète, he would often look out of his flat window at the children playing football in the streets.[3] A bizarre set of circumstances saw him befriend an orphan and all of a sudden he was coaching the kids' football team.

From this, he realised the great pleasure coaching could bring and he was offered a job as an official youth coach. There is a fantastic quote in Jonathan Wilson's *The Names Heard Long Ago* in which Bukovi sums up his feelings as a coach and how it came about: 'Players rarely think about football. I did think. I made up systems, asked coaches, wanted to know. I thought about the ways of training, often unsatisfied with the practices we had. I felt that we needed to work with more of a plan, that what we were doing was an inexcusable improvisation, that coaches didn't recognise anything new and would simply drill in the same thing they did when they were players. What I'm really trying to say is that I always had a magnet drawing me to the coach's calling. A man carries that germ and then gets infected, even though he didn't think about it, or didn't have that firm intention, and he finds peace in the calling that suits him best.'

This germ may have come from the early teachings of John Tait Robertson and Jimmy Hogan and the example set by Hugo Meisl in taking the game to new levels. When Bukovi became Građanski coach, he instantly began looking at new systems and discoursing with other coaches.

Following Herbert Chapman's success at Arsenal, the W-M formation was now the trendy line-up and most teams were deploying this formation. Before Bukovi took over, the previous coach had begun to implement the W-M and the board who hired Bukovi were keen for him to continue on this path. However, Bukovi was not fully convinced by the W-M and, fortunately for him, the board members did not really know much about football, so he blagged his way around the issue. He told them it may take time for his squad to fully grasp the W-M but actually went about training his players to play the Italian-style system known as 'metodo'. Instead of bringing back the centre-half from midfield into defence, it would be the inside-forwards who would drop back. It was, in a roundabout way, a system in between the old 2-3-5 and the W-M. After the season was cancelled in 1935/36, Liverpool were invited over for a friendly match.

This made Bukovi anxious, as he now had to showcase the English method of W-M, which he was supposed to be implementing, against an English side. He feared he would be caught out and that the board would realise he had not been training his team to play the W-M at all. However, Građanski handed Liverpool a humbling 5-1 defeat and it was said that Građanski had given the English side a taste of their own medicine. It was, in fact, more of an Italian recipe which led to the victory. At that time, Liverpool were not one of the best teams in England, but it was still seen as a massive achievement for Građanski and the result brought plaudits from all over the continent. So much so that Građanski were invited to tour England.

Liverpool won the return game 4-0 and Građanski also lost to Wolves, West Ham and Doncaster. Visiting Scotland, they drew 4-4 with Hearts. For some coaches, defeat can always be seen as a positive and, even before the tour, Bukovi had concerns that his team and the European game as a whole were too nice, too passive. The tour convinced him that he needed to change his vision and build a team who played more directly. He invested fully in the W-M, withdrawing his centre-half into defence and detailing the full-backs to deal with the wingers. What he liked about this formation was that it allowed his team to build attacks from their own half. The old passing style he was brought up on relied on too many short passing sequences to outsmart the opponent. He now believed it was more beneficial to advance quickly up the pitch and bypass most of the opposition's defensive structure (counter-attacking). Using the W-M was controversial in Zagreb, as many believed it was a betrayal of the old Danubian way, but Bukovi won a lot of trophies with the system.

A great asset Bukovi had was that he was not a proud person. As the earlier quote shows, he was always happy to listen and implement new ideas and styles. He used these character traits to gain the confidence of his players, too. He could speak a number of languages and all the players respected him and took in his words of advice. As a result of the success he enjoyed at Građanski, his old club Ferencváros would come calling in the summer of 1942, but he rejected them to stay in Zagreb.

* * *

In June 1945, Yugoslavia was invaded and the Communist Party had control. Građanski, along with a number of other clubs, were forced to fold as punishment for playing in the fascist-run league which operated during the war. However, Građanski were effectively rebranded and became Dinamo Zagreb. Bukovi, who was approached by a number of the senior players of this new club, agreed to become coach and their first season, 1945/46, ended up in a showdown against Lokomotivia in a game which decided who would be champions. Analysing and tweaking his trusted W-M formation, Bukovi knew he needed to get an edge over his opponents. He looked at his distinctively average centre-forward, Dragutin Hripko, and requested that he listen to him. As all his players did, Hripko took on board what his manager was asking of him, which was to almost go against everything he had done before as a striker. Bukovi asked Hripko to withdraw, to drop even deeper than Pedernera had done in the 'La Maquina' system. Bukovi not only wanted him to link up the play but to take advantage of the man-marking which was a feature of the W-M formation. With the centre-half having been withdrawn from midfield into the defence in the W-M formation, Bukovi now took his centre-forward completely out of the attacking line and asked him to drop into the space in midfield. This was the starting base for the shift from the W-M to 4-2-4, a formation that would bring huge success to Hungary and joy to all of those who were lucky enough to watch it in motion.

In terms of the recipe for Total Football, at this point we have the Scottish passing style mixed with the 'Scheiberspiel' culture, which was taken to South America, where the mix of youth, patience and a stroke of luck put together a machine-like team who, despite great success, did not last long at the top. Hungary was always a country that continued to compete and, towards the end of the 1940s, some of its exiled footballers were beginning to return home. In 1947, Bukovi returned to the reformed MTK to continue his coaching destiny. Zoltán Opata, one of the great early signings to the MTK side in the illustrious 1920s era, was now a coach plying his trade in Romania, but he was enticed back to his homeland to become Ferencváros coach. Béla Guttmann would also find himself coaching in Hungary in the same year. His story, of course, is a much crazier one, as he had escaped a Nazi concentration camp along with Ernő Egri Erbstein, which is covered in his biography *The Greatest Comeback*. A fascinating character, Guttmann coached 25 teams (officially) and, throughout his career, he was never far from controversy and fantastic tales. He was a fantastic footballing pioneer and his first real success as a manager was with Újpest FC, winning the league and the Mitropa Cup in 1939. After this triumph, his work was halted by the war. Making his comeback in 1945, he managed a few Budapest-based clubs and had a stint in Bucharest before returning to Újpest FC in 1947.

Gyula Mándi, part of the MTK side that won seven consecutive league titles in the 1920s, had also survived the Holocaust thanks to a cunning ploy by a relative. He was freed from a concentration camp in Ukraine when his brother-in-law, György Szomolányi, showed up at the camp looking for workers for his factory and chose Mándi among them. Mándi soon returned to Budapest and, after retiring from the game, was another man infected by the football bug. He had a desire to pass on the messages instilled in him by Jimmy Hogan in his teenage years. What Mándi brought to the game as a player had been revolutionary at the time; as a defender, he tore up the stereotype of being the brute 'stopper' and was one of the first players to play out from the back. This talent was spurred on by Hogan, who wanted all players to be able to play everywhere on the pitch. So, in the late 1940s and early 1950s, many of the famed crop of players who changed the course of modern football 20 years earlier were back in Budapest and ready to carry on what they had started. However, politics and the threat of conflict had still not left the country.

By 1945, the Nazis had been defeated but Budapest had been devastated by a two-month siege in which the whole city was pretty much demolished; around 80 per cent of the buildings in the city were damaged or destroyed, including all seven bridges across the Danube. Following the war,

Hungary became a Soviet satellite state and this impacted on football. During his time in Yugoslavia, Bukovi had seen his club disbanded and re-formed for political reasons. Now, the same happened to the clubs in Budapest. Kispest were re-formed as Budapest Honvéd and became the army team, meaning they could conscript anyone they wanted to come and play for them. MTK were controlled by the secret police, whilst Ferencváros were sanctioned for their alleged links with fascism during the war. As history shows, ruling political parties understand that football can be an integral tool used for their own benefit and it would be no different in post-war Hungary.

In 1949, the obvious choices as national coach were Béla Guttmann or Márton Bukovi. However, neither fitted the bill. Guttmann's character and outspoken demeanour made it almost impossible for the state to hire him. Bukovi was always blunt in his interviews, often giving reporters warnings that he was about to spill some home truths that he just couldn't keep to himself.

The other choice was a man who had imbedded himself within the sports ministry, a man who was seen as someone who possessed a number of communist credentials. His name was Gusztáv Sebes. Born in Budapest, Sebes became a trade union official and moved to Paris as part of his role, working as a fitter at the Renault garage.

During his time in France, he played for the factory's football team, Club Olympique Billancourt. After returning to Hungary in 1927, he went on to play for MTK and Hungaria FC. He then got into the managerial world via a number of Budapest clubs, his main passion being the boardroom. He joined the ministry of sport and worked his way through the ranks, becoming deputy. This, from the state's point of view, made him the perfect man to manage the national team and he was appointed in 1949.

Before looking into how the great 'Aranycsapat' (Golden Team) were built tactically, it is important to note that Sebes's main influence was as a leader rather than a tactician. Sebes believed the secret of success of the great teams to emerge in countries including Italy and Austria was that they had selected groups of players who were familiar with each other rather than picking the best of the bunch from multiple clubs. This is something Spain would do to great effect in 2010, with the majority of their team coming from Real Madrid and Barcelona.

Hungary's selection was also impacted by the political situation – in particular, Honvéd's status as the army club. Honvéd already boasted two fantastic young players named József Bozsik and Ferenc Puskás and it was easy to see why these two would become the core of the national side Sebes was building. It is believed Sebes was the driving force behind the army choosing Kispest to become the army team (Honvéd) and he was effectively allowed to make Honvéd the training camp for the national side. The club poached Zoltán Czibor, Sándor Kocsis and László Budai from Ferencváros. They also signed Gyula Grosics, a goalkeeper, and Gyula Lóránt from their respective clubs, forming a mini national team at club level.

Sebes tried to hide his political beliefs, but this wasn't easy for him, as he was deeply committed to socialist ideology. Whenever there was a big game, the team talk would always be stirred up with a political edge and he was once quoted as saying: 'The fierce struggle between capitalism and socialism took place as much on the football field as anywhere else.' The Hungary team had its manager and the group who would become the 'Golden Team' was gradually being assembled. Sebes was consulting Bukovi and Guttmann over formations and the team would, of course, need a style of play to go with the formation he settled on. The W-M now had many forms and these included the early version of 4-2-4 Bukovi had developed, featuring a deep-lying centre-forward. The formation, tactics and style of the 'Golden Team' would come together like a jigsaw. What made Sebes's team so able to adapt to innovative tactics and formations was one of the fundamentals the Hungarians learned from Hogan – that all players should be able to play in every position for the sake of the team.

Now, combining this individual versatility with the tactical adaptations the game had undergone, Sebes and the coaches made the national team a fluid, attacking outfit. Bukovi was far too independent to join Hungary as an official assistant but Mándi, whom Sebes called upon to bring his brilliant innovations on playing out from the back, was more than happy to take the role, along with former team-mate Opata. Mándi's appointment proved to be a good one. In May 1950, Hungary were defeated 5-3 by Austria; after Mándi became assistant, they went on to win nine games and draw one in the build-up to the 1952 Olympics. Mándi was allowed to experiment and coach from the shadows. The writer Martí Perarnau summed up just how important Mándi was to the modern game, describing him as a great master who was happy to stay in the background but was undoubtedly the brains behind the brilliant football Hungary produced.

As a player, Mándi was cool and calm on the ball; rather than booting it aimlessly upfield, he would opt for short, precise passes, as if he were a midfielder. It is also worth remembering that his full-back partner in that MTK team was Bela Guttmann, so one can only wonder what impact the two of them had on each other. Something we take for granted now is a central defender being able to play football as well as a midfielder; when Pep Guardiola deploys a centre-back in central midfield or when Sergio Busquets drops into centre-back from his usual position in the middle of the park, they make it look natural.

This was born in the head of Mándi and vital to the success of the 'Golden Team'. What was also important in this era was that, with the game as we know it edging closer to becoming 100 years old, the experience and knowledge among players and coaches was, naturally, much greater. Rather than a team being influenced by one revolutionary manager or coach, teams were now being influenced by a number of pioneers and the 'Golden Team' benefited massively from this. Opata, who was a short but sharp striker in his playing days, brought his great experience as a player to his coaching. He did already have experience coaching the Hungarian national team when he was hired as manager in 1936 and took them to the Olympic Games in Berlin, but they were defeated in the first round by Poland.

Whilst Bukovi may take the credit for inspiring Hungary's use of the deep-lying centre-forward, there is no doubt that Opata's influence while coaching the national side was what made the tactic so successful for the 'Golden Team'. He worked tirelessly on the training pitch with Nándor Hidegkuti, Sándor Kocsis and, of course, Ferenc Puskás, one of the all-time greats. It was Hidegkuti who would make the deep-lying centre-forward position famous and his success was down to Opata's coaching. At first, Hidegkuti was not a regular in the team and he had to wait his turn. Péter Palotás was initially the centre-forward but he could not quite grasp how to play the role. Hidegkuti, meanwhile, was aided by having Bukovi as his manager at MTK at the time.

Sebes and his staff set up a nationwide coaching network, meaning relationships were built with all the Hungarian clubs. Sebes would use the clubs for warm-up matches or friendlies before internationals, asking them to adopt the tactics he expected Hungary's opponents to use. He didn't stop there in his quest to perfect his team's preparations. Today, sport science is perhaps even more important than tactics for many clubs, who look to gain an advantage over the opposition by being fitter and stronger athletes with the aid of science. In many ways, this is the antithesis of Total Football, as it places so much emphasis on statistical analysis and pre-planning, taking away the unexpected side of the game. But Sebes would be one of the first coaches to introduce such revolutionary methods to the game of football. This included introducing swimming sessions to increase his players' power and lung capacity. The team bonding sessions he organised took place at art galleries and museums, rather being based around drinking and partying. Sebes also brought in medical professionals to educate the players on the dangers of alcohol and smoking.

His political connections allowed him to secure state-of-the-art sporting facilities for his squad's preparations for the big tournaments. The first of these major competitions would be the 1952 Olympics in Finland and the Hungarian national football team were desperate to showcase the hard work they had put in during the early years under Sebes.

* * *

Going into this tournament, the team was pretty much settled into that which would go on to produce some of the best football the world had ever seen. Puskás was, without question, the best player in the team and was at the heart of it all. He was perhaps the only player who got a slightly free ride when it came to the team attacking and defending as a whole, but he was an extremely intelligent player and a fantastic character. He was a chubby man with a passion for whisky and was frequently caught out off the pitch indulging in activities Sebes would have frowned upon. There are endless great stories about his off-the-pitch antics; these included attending a house party in Glasgow with Scotland star Jim Baxter. He was a lovable character and confident and cocky with it. He was always at the centre of dressing room jokes, like the time he was tricked into eating a banana with the skin on after being given the fruit for the first time in his life.

His talent was second to none and he had a wicked left foot. It is no surprise that FIFA's goal of the year award is named after him. His touch was sublime and he could see things on the pitch that perhaps only Leo Messi could rival. Even allowing for the slight adjustment in how much work he had to get through compared to his team-mates, he was a crucial part of the team's cohesion. Sándor Kocsis, who was the other forward, was also a prolific goalscorer and scored 75 goals in 68 appearances for the national team, including seven hat-tricks and 11 goals at the 1954 World Cup finals. Famous for scoring headers, he was a player who used to great effect the space created by Hidegkuti. Zoltán Czibor was Hungary's outside-left and, in may ways, he was the perfect winger. He had a thunderous shot, a great touch and great pace, which the team took full advantage of.

They were all excellent players but the system itself often helped give the impression they were perfect. The system the Hungarians ended up playing was similar to that of 'La

Maquina', a 3-3-4 with a false nine who would be counted as a midfielder once Hidegkuti cemented his place in the forward line after the Olympics in 1952. One of the midfielders, József Bozsik, was another one of the squad who would stand out. Often listed among the greatest-ever Hungarian players, he wasn't blessed with pace but, operating from quite a deep position, influenced games by combining his great ability at winning the ball with impressive technique and creative flair. Bozsik spent his entire career with Budapest Honvéd, making 477 appearances, and earned 101 international caps.

The 'Golden Team' were blessed with some of the greatest players in the world and, as with 'La Maquina', may never have emerged without a specific crop of players coming together at that precise time. However, you have to feel that both success stories were inevitable because of the circumstances that led up to them. At River Plate, it was the foundation of the academy and the brilliant work it did. In Hungary, a group of the best players from a previous generation arrived at the nation's top clubs to influence and inspire a new generation, all working together to produce what they believed was the best way to become the greatest footballing side in the world – and that is just what they did.

* * *

The Olympic Games in Helsinki in 1952 provided the perfect platform for the emerging Hungarian side and they did not disappoint. After beating Romania 2-1 in the first game and a fantastic 3-0 win over Italy, they followed up with two emphatic victories, hammering Turkey 7-1 and Sweden 6-0. It was the demolition of reigning champions Sweden which would trigger a series of events that would shape the modern game and, without doubt, help open the

eyes of the Dutch to the new ideas this great team brought
to football.

The ripples of excitement over Hungary's football
reached the shores of Britain and, although they were not
in a successful period, the English national team were still
regarded as the most prestigious of opponents. FA secretary
Sir Stanley Rous began negotiations with the Hungarian
authorities and it was later agreed that a friendly between the
two nations would take place at Wembley in November 1953.
Meanwhile, the final of the Olympics pitched Hungary
against Yugoslavia and it was a politically charged occasion.
Yugoslavia had beaten the Soviet Union in the first round
of the Games, a victory which came only four years after a
fall-out between Soviet leader Joseph Stalin and Josip Broz
Tito, the Yugoslav supremo. It was a blow to Soviet pride
and defeat for its satellite state, Hungary, was not an option.
In the event, Puskás and Zoltán Czibor scored a goal each
and the Hungarians took the gold medal with a 2-0 victory.

This team had nowhere near reached their peak, though,
and in a game against Switzerland a few months later, the
final piece in the 'Golden Team' jigsaw would fall into place.
Bukovi now knew that Hidegkuti was ready to become the
deep-lying forward but, against the Swiss, Palotás, a player
who was also playing at MTK under Bukovi, started in
the role.

The Hungarians soon found themselves 2-0 down and
Hidegkuti was brought on before half-time and asked to
play the deep-lying forward role. Something just clicked.
It was 2-2 by half-time and Hungary went on to win 4-2.
Hidegkuti got himself a goal, but it was the impact he had
in the deep-lying role that was remarkable. He was so good
in the air, he had great finesse and could see the picture of

the pitch and the options available to him. The role he was given brought the best out of his attributes. He was a play-making centre-forward, just as Matthias Sindelar had been. However, this was a step up again from what the 'Paper Man' and Austria achieved. The tactical evolution of the game had now allowed this Hungarian side to produce a team so fluid in both attack and defence that they appeared unbeatable.

Indeed, between 1950 and 1956, they would be beaten only once and that was in the World Cup Final. In 69 games in that period, they recorded 58 wins and ten draws.

This success was created through collaboration. The players – most notably Puskás, Hidegkuti and Bozsik – would spend the opening sequence of a game reading the patterns of play so that they could decipher where the opponents' weaknesses were and how they were going to exploit them. The players had been conditioned – through training, coaching and playing matches – to think for themselves about how they wanted to play the game rather than simply doing as they were told. This is a trait that Total Football teams seem to have.

None more so than the Dutch, whose on-field coaches were led by Johan Cruyff, who was continually pointing, shouting instructions and directing his team-mates. In effect, Hungary had six forwards on the pitch but, as Hidegkuti once stated: 'Though all six of us could attack, we never played in a line formation. If I went forward, Puskás dropped back. If Kocsis drifted wide, Bozsik moved into the middle. There was always space to play the ball into.' Hidegkuti also alluded to another part of their game which would make up a large part of the Total Football ethos: 'We constantly changed positions, so where we lined up at kick-off was irrelevant.' The 'Golden Team' enhanced the W-M formation whilst implementing elements of the more direct approach, which was still being used in Britain, and it was all underpinned by the basic principles Hogan fed into Hungarian football earlier in the century.

After the win against Switzerland, all eyes began to look ahead to the prestige friendly against England. Before that, though, Hungary had another final to play, this time against Italy in the Central European Championship, a competition which was played in a league format. In May 1953, Hungary travelled to Rome and comfortably beat Italy 3-0 with two goals from Puskás and one from Hidegkuti. They now had six months to prepare for the big game against England. Sebes, known for his attention to detail, didn't let anything slip in his preparations for this one.

Exploiting his political connections, he was allowed to co-opt army club Honvéd for practice matches in which they were ordered to adopt the tactics and style of play typical of England. He also obtained English balls, which absorbed more moisture during a game, becoming heavier. Sebes even had smoke wafted over the pitch during training in a bid to replicate the foggy conditions which were common in London at the time. Nothing was left to chance. Sebes organised a friendly against Sweden to take place ten days before the game at Wembley.

He was perhaps hoping for a confidence-boosting repeat of the 6-0 rout at the Olympics, but it did not go to plan and Hungary could only manage a 2-2 draw. The heavy English ball slowed down their play and their performance prompted a barrage of abuse from the Hungarian media. Winning 18-0 in a training match against Sebes's old factory team in Paris on their way to England may have restored some confidence.

The match of the century

England, who had never been beaten on home soil by a team from outside the UK and Ireland, were not at their greatest at the time of this game, but England was still regarded as the birthplace of the game and, as a result, were seen as the team to beat. Many strong national teams had tried and failed. England were still unbeaten at home against continental sides and no nation other than Scotland had beaten them at Wembley. Despite their impressive run, Hungary were not too confident of getting a result, which was probably reflected in the extraordinary lengths Sebes was going to in his preparations for the game. In many ways, the team had already been completed, tactically and personnel-wise. The 'Golden Team' had arrived, but this offered the opportunity to announce it to the world if they got it right. In front of a 100,000 Wembley crowd on 25 November 1953, the world of football changed forever. It only took 45 seconds. Bozsik slid through a pass to Hidegkuti and, after a lovely feint to beat an England defender, he smashed the ball into the far left top corner to make it 1-0 to Hungary.

England were as arrogant as they had been in the previous years when pretenders to their self-proclaimed status as 'masters of football' stepped up against them. They had got away with it in the past, but this was to be a different story altogether. England were not only going to be blown away, they would also be shown how far behind they were falling in the world game. This was even evident in the warm-up before kick-off as the England players opted for the odd stretch and a chat among themselves, something akin to a Sunday league team's warm-up. Hungary, meanwhile, prepared with a revolutionary routine, having earlier had a tactical talk from Sebes lasting four hours. England's defeat wasn't just a wake-up call; this was a realisation for the country who claimed to be the creators of the game that they had been overtaken by Hungary and the modern coaching and tactical styles that Hungarians and other countries were developing.

Shortly after the opening goal, England managed to equalise and it briefly seemed the game may take a different course, wiping out any need for the English to be worried about the state of their football. However, that did not last long. Hidegkuti got his second and Puskás scored the game's best goal when he chopped and dragged the ball back past the England captain Billy Wright, smashing it into the net as Wright went flying past him in the wrong direction. The assist for this goal came from left-winger Czibor crossing the ball from the right flank, showing just how fluid this side was. Bozsik added a fourth before England grabbed a second before the half-time whistle. This game is available to view on the internet and I beg you to watch it. You can clearly see how all the training Sebes had had his team doing paid off; the Hungarians looked fitter, stronger and faster than their counterparts and they created chance after chance.

What is also great about the footage is how the English commentator is left in a state of constant confusion by Hungarian players popping up in different positions all over the pitch. The W-M that England so inevitably used was far too rigid to cope with the fluidity of the Hungarian formation. In the second half, Bozsik added a fifth and Hidegkuti completed his hat-trick with a lovely volley. Alf Ramsey converted a penalty for England and the game finished 6-3 to Hungary. The margin of victory could have been anything Hungary wanted, as it is clear they took their foot off the pedal towards the end, keeping the ball from the English as if to say 'this is our game now'.

Sebes stated that his side played a socialist brand of football built on the cohesion and teamwork of the players and staff involved – the exact opposite of what the English game was based on. This is illustrated by footage of the kick-off after Puskás's goal. England take the kick-off and a forward runs at the Hungarian team in a manner you would expect to see in kids' football; he is easily dispossessed and Hungary launch a counter-attack, the ball flying out to the right wing and László Budai drags a shot wide. The game was filled with these moments. To really round things off in a full circle, Jimmy Hogan was sitting in the stands that day. Ironically, he was a guest of honour of the Hungarians. The great football the English public had just witnessed could have been their own if they had embraced Hogan. Instead, he took it to the rest of the world. Sebes rubbed it in after the match, saying: 'We played football as Jimmy Hogan taught us.' Sebes went on to say that, when the history of Hungarian football was written, Hogan's name should be in gold letters.

Hungary's triumph was also, of course, a great propaganda tool for the Hungarian Communist Party. Although the political situation had helped Sebes in his work with the national team, nationalisation had not benefited the Hungarian people. In the early 1950s, the standard of living fell alarmingly and, with curbs on religion and education being tightly controlled, life in Hungary was brutal. For many people, football was the perfect escape, the one activity that united the country. When England were invited to Hungary for a rematch in May 1954, the excitement for the game was immeasurable. More than a million people applied for tickets to the game in Budapest, showing how much the Hungarian people needed football in their lives. With a crowd in excess of 100,000 – the official figure is thought to be an underestimate – this really was a game that no one wanted to miss.

There are tales that fans tied their tickets to carrier pigeons once inside the ground so they could fly and deliver them to friends and family outside the stadium for them to re-use. Hungary did not disappoint all those fans who worked so hard to get into the stadium. It would be another hammering for England and the scoreline this time better represented just how far apart the two nations were when it came to football. Hungary won 7-1. The same system and tactics, Hidegkuti causing mayhem amongst the English. Another modern trait that Hungary displayed during these years and showcased in this game was the importance of encouraging goalkeeper Grosics to leave his box and act as a sweeper. In possession, the forward line would move towards their own goal rather than the opposition's, the exact opposite to what most other teams in the world were doing. Sebes constantly stressed that his team played a system that was much bigger than the individual and the system was at its pinnacle against England. This game is also easily available online to watch back and it could be seen as just an extension of the first meeting, England kicking off and running straight into the Hungarians, who launch attack after attack. The pictures available of this game also capture just what it meant to the locals.

* * *

The rout of England provided the perfect preparation for the upcoming 1954 World Cup in Switzerland, for which Hungary were strong favourites.

Hungary qualified without having to play a game because Poland dropped out. Unbeaten since 1950, the 'Golden

Team' wanted to get their hands on the golden prize. It was a bizarre set-up for this World Cup. The group stage was organised so that two seeded teams were drawn alongside two unseeded teams and the teams with the same ranking did not play each other, meaning each team only played two group games.

A 9-0 win over South Korea was the perfect start for Hungary. In their second game, they played against a West Germany team who had foreseen their future and decided to play a weakened side to make sure they were fresh for a play-off against Turkey, which seemed likely if they suffered an expected reverse at the feet of the Hungarians. Hungary won 8-3. However, West Germany would make a huge impact on Hungary's tournament in that game when an horrific tackle left Puskás with a small fracture in his ankle, forcing him to miss the next game, the quarter-final against Brazil.

In the 'Battle of Berne', as it would become known, Hungary beat Brazil 4-2 but the game was marred by violence and fighting between players, officials and fans. Sebes needed stitches for his injuries and Pinheiro accused Puskás of glassing him with a bottle. After Hungary took a 2-0 lead after only seven minutes with their flying, free-flowing football, Brazil lost their heads and the Hungarians joined them. English referee Arthur Ellis, who was determined to see that the game finished, admitted later that he probably should have abandoned it, as the behaviour of the players was simply ridiculous. Somehow, the game only ended up with three dismissals. Without Puskás, Hungary had made it through to the semi-finals where they would have to beat Uruguay, who had never lost a World Cup match in their history at that point. Having ended England's unbeaten home record against continental teams, Hungary now looked to end another unbeaten record. This, though, was much more of a challenge. Again missing the injured Puskás, Hungary led for the majority of the game, with an early goal from Zoltán Czibor and a second from Hidegkuti early in the second half. Uruguay replied by launching attack after attack and Hungary had to show their abilities as a defensive outfit more than they ever had under Sebes.

This game was the exact opposite to the quarter-final against Brazil. It was perhaps the greatest showing of football there has ever been at a World Cup. This was two teams playing a similar style, albeit with differences in tactics and formations. Uruguay fought back in the second half to level the game at 2-2 and force extra-time. This would be where Sebes's innovative training methods would prove to be a difference-maker, as it was evident that the Hungarians were much fitter than their opponents as they went on to win 4-2. They had beaten the two top teams in South America and, in the final, would face West Germany, a team they had already beaten comfortably in the group stage. What could possibly go wrong?

Puskás passed himself fit to play, despite clear concerns over his fitness, and scored after eight minutes. Two minutes later, Hungary were 2-0 up and it looked like they would cruise to a much-deserved World Cup triumph. After 20 minutes, however, the West Germans had battled their way back into the game and drawn level. Then came a mistake that would also haunt the Netherlands 20 years later; the Hungarians appeared to take their foot off the gas, airing an arrogance that they knew they were far superior to the opposition. They fell into a false sense of security and this, coupled with some rotten bad luck, allowed West Germany to pull off perhaps the most astonishing victory in a World in Brussels, losing and going out of the tournament 6-5 on aggregate. The players were unsure whether to return to Budapest and organised a tour of Europe and Brazil to delay their decision even longer. When they finally arrived back in Europe, the players parted ways and many looked for opportunities outside Hungary. Kocsis and Czibor headed for Catalonia and signed for Barcelona.

Puskás also went to Spain, signing for Real Madrid, where he would become even more of a household name. This would be Puskás's only other official club team in his career, although he did play a few unofficial games for Espanyol in Barcelona after refusing to return to Hungary following the tour with Honvéd. He would later make an appearance for English non-league side South Liverpool after he retired, playing in a charity match which attracted a sell-out crowd of 10,000. Remarkably, he played for the Spanish national team a handful of times before his retirement. He was, of course, also present on the pitch at Hampden in the famous European Cup Final against Frankfurt in which he scored four goals. He is a player that many older fans can still remember from their early days of watching the game. His most current influence on the game came as a result of his spell as a manager in Australia during which he coached a young player named Ange Postecoglou who went on to manage Celtic and took over as Tottenham manager in 2023, immediately winning the hearts of the English press with his style of football. It is a style he credits to his time being coached by the great Ferenc Puskás.

* * *

The 'Golden Team' had been demolished, broken down and split back across the world. This was a team built on many

Cup Final, a miracle of sorts. Hungary were visibly not as flowing and ruthless as they could be, but were still creating chances. However, due to poor finishing and some amazing saves from German goalkeeper Toni Turek, Hungary could not find a winner.

They had 26 shots in the game but had only their two early goals to show for it. In the 84th minute, with the game still deadlocked at 2-2, the West Germans went ahead with a goal from Helmut Rahn. Puskás thought he had equalised in the 88th minute, but the goal was ruled out for offside. In the final minute, there seemed to be a clear foul on Kocsis in the penalty area, but nothing was given. Remarkably, Sepp Herberger was once again the villain in the story we are following. He was sharp enough to try and counter the impact of Hidegkuti by assigning Horst Eckel to man-mark him and Hidegkuti wasn't as influential as he usually was, although he did hit the post with a chance that could easily have gone in on another day. There is no doubt that luck played a huge part in the defeat and Hungary perhaps suffered more from that than fatigue or mind games from the opposition. Despite their fantastic run, Hungary had lost the game that mattered most. Sebes suffered the brunt of the abuse from back home. Bizarrely, he did seem to change the line-up for the final, swapping his wide players in a bid to confuse the Germans.

The inclusion of Puskás was also controversial, as there were major question marks about just how fit he was. There have subsequently been claims that the Germans had doped their players with performance-enhancing methamphetamine. But, whatever the reasons, Hungary had lost, just as the Dutch would do at the same stage when showcasing their own wonderful brand of football. There were eerily similar problems in the Hungarians' build-up to the final to those the Dutch suffered in 1978, when their team was delayed on the way to the stadium. The same happened to the Hungarians when the police denied their bus access to the ground, so the players had to get out and fight their way through the crowds to get to the stadium. The Hungarian people did not take kindly to the final defeat and the players had to go into virtual hiding when they returned, with angry fans wanting answers as to why they had not brought back the Jules Rimet Trophy. Sebes himself never fully recovered from it all; his standing within the government was supposed to be enhanced by winning the World Cup, which would have been regarded as a great triumph for the communist rulers, but the defeat exposed vulnerabilities that the political leaders didn't want to admit. Fans who tried to voice their opinions on the disappointment of not bringing home the World Cup were usually silenced. The 'Aranycsapat' had lost their spirit and the energy they received from their fans. The country was being gripped even tighter by the Hungarian People's Republic rulers and revolution was inevitable.

* * *

The World Cup defeat and the unease at home did not derail the 'Golden Team' and they carried on playing their great football for a further two years, going another 18 games unbeaten. This spell included two particularly notable victories. In 1955, they faced Scotland at Hampden Park in front of 113,000 fans. Hungary won the game 4-2 despite Scotland giving a much better account of themselves against the 'Golden Team' than the English had. Scotland outside-right Johnny MacKenzie produced some fantastic wing play,

tormenting Mihály Lantos throughout, but the [...] had just too much for the Scots. On 23 Septem[...] the 'Golden Team' threw themselves into the [...] the mood of civil unrest amongst many Hungaria[...] they played the Soviet Union at Lenin Central Stad[...] Moscow in front of a 105,000 crowd.

The Soviets had never lost a game on home soi[...] their record was ruined as Hungary ran out 1-0 winr[...] Many of the golden generation of players were now agei[...] but they dented the pride of the Soviet communist hierarch[...] aiding the ongoing swing towards a revolution back home[...] Sebes was relieved of his duties and, in 1956, Bukovi finally took over as manager. Mándi was also asked to leave his post as assistant. Sebes retained his place on the political landscape of the sporting world in Hungary and went on to be vice president of UEFA in the 1960s. The Hungary team, along with their staff, were being dismantled and they would eventually meet their demise amid the political turmoil in Hungary. On 23 October 1956, university students gathered in Budapest to protest against the socialist state run by Mátyás Rákosi. When a group of students who entered the parliament building to make demands for civil reforms were detained by the state police, protesters gathered outside demanded their release and the State Protection Authority opened fire on them, killing several.

Budapest was no longer safe. Conflict followed and, by the end of the uprising, more than 2,500 lives were lost and 200,000 Hungarians had fled the country, including many of the famous 'Golden Team'. As most of them were playing for Budapest Honvéd, they were in Bilbao for a match in the newly formed European Cup when the uprising kicked off. Instead of returning home, they played the home leg

of the foundations followed in this book so far, foundations that began in their own country thanks to Jimmy Hogan and John Tait Robertson and were adapted by the Austrians, who added a culture of entertainment. When River Plate built their academy around the style, they needed it to be more competitive and free-flowing, so added an abundance of pace and attacking threat. What the Hungarians brought to it was amazing in that they kept the freedom but built an environment in which the players were trained and almost conditioned to absorb the best of the latest techniques, allowing them to play the great football they did. Sebes was a political figure, but he used this power both ways; to impress the powers in charge of the country but also to gain an edge when negotiating what would be best for his side. Sebes often referred to his team's style as 'socialist football' in a reference to the fact that all the players had to play their part for the team to work as a whole. The style was certainly marvellous and this is why they were loved. Even now, watching the games in black and white, you can feel yourself admiring the Hungarians like it was a live game. I just can't imagine what this must have been like to witness live. It was enough to influence the world of football until the current day.

The connection to the fans was thanks to Mándi and Opata; they understood how to implement the style on the players and the development of the tactics came from their experiences as players. Bukovi and Guttmann also played their part. These four all learnt directly from Hogan himself and they clubbed together and created the 'Golden Team', arguably the greatest footballing side ever. But, just like the great Total Football creators from the Netherlands, they missed out on the greatest prize of them all, the World Cup. Did that really matter? It would still be nearly 20 years until Total Football was fully born. What happened in those intervening years? Did anyone try to recreate the 'Aranycsapat' or was it deemed a failure after losing the World Cup? And how did the Dutch manage to get infected by the germ of this style that was somehow waiting for them to develop into the finished article?

Part Five

The Birth of Total Football

WE ARE nearly at the end; we have almost reached the point at which Total Football was born and produced for the world to see. The achievements of Ajax and the Netherlands whilst playing their Total Football has been covered by many better writers than me; there have been fantastic books and documentaries and the tales and stories related to the Total Football philosophy would easily fill another book. Now that all the origins and ideas have been covered, what could be left that would lead to Total Football being produced? Was it a case of Rinus Michels stumbling across the old coaching books of Jimmy Hogan and following the trail left by him so that he could produce a playing style fit for the teams he was managing?

There is no doubt he would have been familiar with many of the names covered so far, but what makes Total Football so great is that many of the people involved in producing it may never have heard of 'La Maquina' or the 'Wunderteam' or even Hogan, but they have built a footballing ideology which seems to cover all the things they also believed in. An extension of this idea is that, if you could ask Michels and Johan Cruyff if they believed these styles match what they created, they may have disagreed entirely. There were other teams that so nearly produced the same style of football at a similar time; Valeriy Lobanovskyi and his Kyiv side and a more bizarre attempt in Italy from Tommaso Maestrelli. Something was missing from those sides, something or someone the Dutch had that allowed the puzzle to be completed. That final piece of the puzzle is, of course, Hendrik Johannes Cruijff or, as he is better known, Johan Cruyff.

He signed for Ajax in 1957 aged ten. The final route on this journey is to follow those who influenced and built Cruyff into the player, manager, adviser and critic who would arguably impact the game of football more than anyone else, more than the pioneers who created the game, more than any of the people already mentioned. Cruyff showed all the traits and beliefs of many of the characters included in this book and he would also grow up playing the game on the streets of the neighbourhood in which he grew up. Just as the grunds of Budapest or the potreros of Argentina produced previous greats, Cruyff would learn the game on the concrete streets of Akkerstraat in Betondorp, Amsterdam, the recreation ground near his house and the car park next to the Ajax stadium.

From a young age, everything revolved around football. When he walked to school, he would practice football with a tennis ball. As Auke Kok writes in *Johan Cruyff: Always On the Attack*, Cruyff would be challenged by older children during street games to hit a lamp-post ten metres away and he always succeeded. He hated losing. He was the local problem child to adults and a hero to the children, always with a ball at his feet and when he was dribbling with it, no one could get near him.[18] If there was any chance of him losing a game organised amongst his friends and local children, the ball would be picked up and off Johan would go. Cruyff once claimed that losing affected him deep inside. If there was a prize up for grabs, he would come to life and make sure he won it. His father, Manus, was a massive football fan, which was not common in their neighbourhood. In Akkerstraat, you could see the stadium from the comfort of your own home, but few went there. To this community, football was nothing; it was the opposite of building an education or a career.

Perhaps this is why some adults hated Cruyff so much, as he was already beginning to influence the local children with his love for football. Once they moved to the area, Manus loved Ajax and his son followed suit. At the tender age of 12, Cruyff lost his father to heart failure. This shattered his world and, from then on, Cruyff was drawn to father figures. Henk Angel would become Cruyff's new father figure at home; Cruyff knew Henk as he had been involved with Ajax since 1945 and was always to be found near or inside the stadium and would often look the other way when Cruyff and his pals played football in the gym at the stadium.

Henk was what would be classed today as a kit man, but he contributed to many factors of the club to aid the now professional footballers of Ajax. Cruyff would often help Henk at the stadium, pumping up balls or tending to the pitch. During all this time spent with Henk and at the stadium, Cruyff was absorbing all the tales from Henk and slowly absorbing Ajax into his DNA. His first real father figure in football would be his youth trainer, Jany van der Veen. He was a trainer and former Ajax player; he was also the link between Jack Reynolds and the foundations he built at Ajax and the Ajax of Total Football.

By the time the Hungarian 'Golden Team' had been dismantled, a lot of work had already been done at Ajax, the main club in the capital of the Netherlands, in terms of planting the seeds that would grow into Total Football. This was done by Englishman Jack Reynolds, who is sometimes referred to as the father of the club due to his pioneering ideas and the foundations he put in place during his long stint as manager, which lasted a total of 27 years, albeit interrupted by spells away from the club for various reasons. Reynolds born in Bury, Manchester, and followed a similar path to Hogan. They were of a similar age – Reynolds being a year older – and both had average playing careers followed by long careers in coaching and management. Whilst Hogan managed to get his name known all over the world and influenced football globally, too, Reynolds focused his attention on the city of Amsterdam – and what a change he made.

His mind was filled with the same ideas as Hogan, inspired by the Scottish passing game, but he could not catch a break in England, so moved to Switzerland in 1912. After a couple of successful years, he was approached to become the manager of the German national team. This opportunity was taken away from him by the outbreak of the First World War. Instead, he headed to Amsterdam in 1915 and, armed with a vision of how to train and build a football team, Reynolds set about turning Ajax, a small club who had never won anything in Dutch football, into one of the best sides the country had to offer.

Reynolds spent a brief spell as the Netherlands national coach in 1920 and then worked at Blaauw Wit, another Amsterdam-based club, in 1925 after a falling-out with the Ajax board. Reynolds made Amsterdam his home, running a cigar shop alongside his football work, as Ajax were not a professional outfit. Many credit Reynolds with planting the seed of Total Football at Ajax, with the others along the way watering the plant and making sure it grew. Reynolds did this by encouraging a similar attacking style of play at Ajax to the style Hogan brought to Hungarian football, but on a more subtle level. Reynolds's football was still very much an English style, with a focus on aggressive wingers, through whom most attacks would come. It was the training methods Reynolds implemented at Ajax that would really impact the club's future. A club who would become world renowned for their coaching and would be the gold standard in the 1990s, began with small, simple drills that Reynolds designed and which focused not only around technique, but also fitness.

As Roldán did in Argentina, Reynolds recognised the importance of building a youth academy and training the young players in the same way as the first team would benefit the club in a massive way. The football Reynolds was trying to create may not have been on a par with that of 'La Maquina', but the fact that this set-up was in place so early was integral. The club's academy would go on to become perhaps the most famous in the world of football, a reputation it still holds today, and there is no doubt that it was these early ideas implemented by the Englishman that allowed Total Football to be created. We know from the previous chapters that the creation of such football styles relied on a number of factors, including luck and an exceptional crop of players; when examining the trajectory under Reynolds, Ajax were beginning to tick a lot of the required boxes.

Reynolds's first stint at the club brought him great success in building Ajax into a force at the top of the league. When he returned in 1927, after three years away, he had to go about a rebuilding of sorts to get them back to the heights he had them at before he left. The fact he achieved this shows just how good a manager he was.

During this second stint, war would again put a spanner in the works. Reynolds was picked up by the Germans in June 1940 and sent to prison camps in the Netherlands, Poland and, finally, France before being exchanged in a prisoner of war transfer, returning to Manchester in 1944. During his time in detention, Reynolds was still able to influence Ajax. As detailed in Simon Kuper's book *Ajax, The Dutch, The War*, he was able to submit his technical tips, as they became known, and these would feature in the club magazine, *Ajax-Niewws*. The magazine regularly published updates on Reynolds's situation whilst he was under arrest. Once he was freed, Reynolds soon returned to Amsterdam and asked for his old job back. It did not take much negotiating and he was reinstated as the club's trainer.[17]

During the 1946/47 season, Reynolds had a player in his ranks called Marinus Jacobus Hendricus Michels or, as you and me know him, Rinus Michels. He had joined the youth set-up founded by Reynolds in 1940. Due to the war, many youth leagues and teams were put on hold and Michels had to serve in the army. French club Lille were interested in signing the youngster but he remained in Amsterdam and resumed his football career in 1946. He made his debut in June of that year against ADO Den Haag, getting his chance because of an injury to a team-mate and repaying Reynolds's faith by scoring five goals in an 8-3 victory. Far from being a technical maestro as a player, Michels was more of a brute, known more for his heading ability and strength than his skill and technique.

The significance of the year Michels spent playing under Reynolds can be regarded in the same light as the time Gyula Mándi and Hirschl had playing under Hogan. The success and progressive style of football Reynolds brought could not be compared with the football the Hungarians would produce in the 1950s, but it was cut from the same cloth, so there is no doubt that it sparked something inside Michels.

Reynolds retired at the end of the 1946/47 season but he continued to live in Amsterdam and would no doubt still have had a say in what was going on at Ajax. Between 1946 and 1958, Michels was a regular in an Ajax side which carried on playing in the style laid down by Reynolds. Michels made 264 appearances, scoring 122 goals. More than a decade after Reynolds left, just as the club were slipping back towards the abyss they found themselves in before he arrived, Ajax would turn to another Englishman. His name was Vic Buckingham and, if Reynolds was the father of Ajax, I propose that Buckingham was the godfather.

* * *

When Reynolds retired, Van der Veen was seen as the guardian of what the Englishman had created. This is a vital moment, as many of the teams mentioned earlier seem to have came to an abrupt end when there was no one to carry on the torch. Van der Veen was brave enough to follow the example led by Reynolds. He praised intelligent, attacking play and ensured that the club concentrated on nurturing technically skilful players rather than those who relied on brute strength. He also carried on the tradition Ajax would become famous for by using homegrown players. Van der Veen insisted his players be brave on the ball, with an emphasis on thoughtful passing. He focused his training sessions on teaching his players the best way to receive the ball so they could easily make the next pass. He forced his players to navigate difficult games by playing controlled possession football rather than allowing panic and aggression to overtake them. Cruyff was now playing under him and he was growing in the same mould as the club was growing. In his autobiography, Cruyff says of Ajax's first European Cup triumph in 1971: 'It was simple – it was a combination of talent, technique and discipline, which were all things that we had been working on at Ajax, even before Rinus Michels had arrived.'[19]

Van der Veen lived on the outskirts of Betondorp and, had he not loved football himself, would have been one of the adults who considered the young Cruyff a nuisance. Instead, he watched from the comfort of his own home as Cruyff, who was eight years old at the time, played street football. Van der Veen noted how well Cruyff could dribble with the ball so close to his feet and, a couple of years later, Cruyff would end up signing for the club.

Van der Veen, who was associated with Ajax for most of his life, had joined the club as a player in 1939. Soon afterwards, Reynolds was arrested and detained by the Germans, but Van der Veen carried on playing for Ajax and was still there when the Englishman returned to lead the successful post-war period. Van der Veen was an integral member of the midfield in a team in which he played alongside Rinus Michels in the second half of his career, but he retired in 1948 due to an injury which ended his career after only 150 appearances. As a trainer, Van der Veen embraced the personal coaching element of the role, which is perhaps something the great River Plate academy lacked. Ajax became famous for teaching their youth players respect and innovation. Cruyff, who was desperate for a father figure, was not only being coached football by Van der Veen but also the values expected of someone in the Ajax family. These values undoubtedly shaped the Total Football

Ajax would go on to play. Cruyff said what he learned under Van der Veen 'was the perfect example of how the Ajax life was, one that compensated for the education that I wouldn't be getting at school'.[19] Van der Veen was dedicated to teaching ball mastery and staging training sessions that always involved a ball.

With the development of modern coaching, the fundamentals are often skipped; kids are taught about pressing and complex tactics before they learn how to master the ball. It seems that coaching has gone from zero in Hogan's era to missing all the basics and heading straight to what Pep Guardiola does in his training sessions. Van der Veen understood the importance of controlling, passing, heading, dribbling and shooting. Drills would be performed methodically and repetitively until all the youth players he trained could master the ball; then would come the tactics, taught by coaches who were all reading from the same sheet. How highly Van der Veen thought of the young Cruyff is illustrated by a story from when he was only 14 and Van der Veen went to watch the sixth team of the Ajax senior set-up, known as Ajax 6. The team would generally get a good humbling and, on this particular occasion, they were missing a number of players and only had ten available to start the game. The coaches approached Van der Veen, asking him if he knew of any players who could step in. Almost as if it was planned, Cruyff appeared on his bike. Van der Veen turned to him and told him that if went off to fetch his boots from his nearby home, he would get a game. Cruyff played and, thanks to him, Ajax 6 won 6-0. Van der Veen was admonished by the bosses of Ajax, as they felt there was no reason for a 14-year-old to be playing senior football, but the episode showed how great Cruyff was to become.

Of course, it was not just Cruyff that Van der Veen taught as a youngster. The team who went on to win a hat-trick of European Cups between 1971 and 1973 included Piet Keizer, Wim Suurbier, Johan Neeskens and Ruud Krol, who all benefited from the guidance of Van der Veen. Keizer, who some claim was just as good, if not better, than Cruyff, was like a brother to Johan. Keizer – like Cruyff, a fantastic dribbler and a heavy smoker – would mentor Johan. Cruyff saw Keizer, who was four years older, as an idol and someone whose play he wanted to replicate. His other hero, Fraas Wilkes, had recently retired and never played for Ajax; Cruyff had to wait until the national team played at the Ajax stadium to catch a glimpse of him. By the mid-1960s, the teenage Cruyff was edging ever closer to the first team of Ajax.[18]

Vic Buckingham arrived as manager in 1959 and would act as yet another footballing father figure for Cruyff. When Cruyff was still in his youth team days, Buckingham would ensure he was given extra meals in a bid to help him gain some weight. As a player, Buckingham spent almost all his career at Tottenham Hotspur as a defensive player, playing either at centre-half or left-half. His career was pretty mundane; Spurs were in Division Two between 1935 and 1949 and, although he racked up more than 200 appearances, Buckingham never played top-flight football. However, towards the end of his career, he was involved in the early stages of the famous team who would go on to win the Second Division and First Division titles back-to-back under the influential push-and-run style Arthur Rowe brought to English football.

Somewhat ahead of its time, Rowe's possession-based football caught the big clubs in England on their heels. Once again, in Buckingham's case, the country's stubbornness towards different styles of football may have contributed to driving one of the most forward-thinking coaches, who could have helped shape English football for decades to come, to express his style overseas.

Buckingham began his management career at a few amateur teams and led Oxbridge-based Pegasus to an FA Amateur Cup Final victory in 1951 in front of a capacity crowd at Wembley. His first job in the professional game was at Bradford Park Avenue in Division Three North before being propelled into the top flight when he became West Bromwich Albion manager in 1953. This would coincide with the Hungarians humbling England in their own backyard and you have to wonder what Buckingham took from that game, as there is no doubt he must have been influenced by it when you consider the trajectory of his career after it.

West Brom became one of the country's most successful sides and won the FA Cup in 1954. The 1953/54 season could have been an historic one, as they came close to becoming the first English club to do the double, finishing as runners-up behind Wolves in the league after leading the title race at one point. The FA Cup win came in what was described as an entertainingly open and attacking game against Preston North End and, other than winning the 1954 Charity Shield, would be his last major honour with Albion.

He managed to keep West Brom at the top of the English game, narrowly missing out on another trip to the FA Cup Final in 1957. Bobby Robson played under Buckingham and, given what he went on to achieve as a manager, this is a pointer towards just how big an influence Buckingham had on the game. It was Buckingham's desire to coach and inspire that would drive him away from the comfort of one of

England's top clubs to an almost amateur Ajax Amsterdam. Buckingham had attempted to change the mentality of football in England while at West Brom. As a coach, he was way ahead of his time – arguably by 70 years – but this wasn't appreciated in England. The move to Ajax would have been seen at the time as a major step down and bizarre choice. Buckingham, however, did not see it that way. He may well have known what was being built there and been aware of the foundations laid by Reynolds. Buckingham appears to have shared the same beliefs as Van der Veen, who was deep into his coaching role at the point Buckingham headed for Amsterdam. It appears Buckingham's attitude was that, being so totally invested in his way of playing, he would take his ideas elsewhere if English football was not prepared to listen.

He chose the Netherlands and a city where similar ideas were already being worked on. He led Ajax to the league title, as well as the national cup, although in later years he played down his part in this, insisting that the players he inherited already had the desired basic skills to play his way and that he just had to mould them as a team and teach them about his possession-based football. The foundations he spoke of were, of course, those laid by Reynolds and enhanced by Van der Veen. What Buckingham was creating was not just a beast at domestic level. He undoubtedly laid the foundations for Ajax's European domination, something he would always play down. Buckingham created a fantastic side at Ajax, but he still felt frustrated that the game in England would not follow the path the continental game was taking. So he left Ajax and returned to England to try again.

He took over at Sheffield Wednesday. In the three seasons he was at the helm, he managed three consecutive sixth-place finishes. Perhaps most notably – and especially in relation to Buckingham's future – was a run to the quarter-finals of the Inter-Cities Fairs Cup. Wednesday lost 4-3 to FC Barcelona, a club who were enjoying life at the summit of European football having been involved in the European Cup Final the season before. Barcelona chiefs noted the name of Vic Buckingham that day after admiring his team's modern style of football. When, in 1964, his contract at Hillsborough was not renewed, he found himself looking for a new club. Wednesday's decision to part ways with Buckingham was overshadowed by the club's involvement in a betting scandal which led to three Wednesday players being found guilty and sentenced to prison terms. There was no suggestion Buckingham was involved but the club believed he did not possess the correct qualities to impose the sort of strict working environment in which such behaviour would be prevented. So off he went, back to Amsterdam for the 1964/65 season.

On 25 October 1964, Ajax were due to play a friendly against Helmondia '55 and, after a poor start to the season, they needed a confidence booster. Their disappointing start was largely influenced by the absence of Piet Keizer, who had suffered an horrific head injury that March. Keizer had come close to dying when he was injured in a challenge with an opposition defender and he was still recovering when the new season got under way. For the Helmondia '55 friendly, Cruyff travelled with the first team for the first time and the plan was to ease him in. He had a mundane game and did nothing to suggest to the fans how brilliant he would become. However, this would not be the case when he made his first proper start in a league game three weeks later. Cruyff was named in the squad to travel to GVAV (who would become FC Groningen).

He was nervous and tense as he sat on the train which left Amsterdam. Moments after a pre-match meal of steak was planted in front of him, Buckingham approached and told Cruyff this was to be the day when he made his first start in the Premier Division. GVAV were a decent side and this was going to be a tough game in a hostile environment in front of 16,000 people. Cruyff, who wore the number eight jersey, was battered by the home fans. They heckled and hurled abuse at Cruyff and his team-mates.

The home fans became even more aggravated when the skinny, unknown teenager began to dish out instructions to his team-mates, waving his arms and acting as the leader of the team. Cruyff was being mocked by the fans but he continued to play his own game and did not shy away from receiving the ball as much as he could. In *Always On the Attack*, author Kok describes how Cruyff was nervous and scared before the game, sneaking a quick cigarette in the showers so his manager couldn't see him, but was then able to settle himself and perform on the pitch as if he was a veteran who had done all this a thousand times. Ajax were defeated 3-1 that day and Cruyff managed to get the consolation goal after converting a tap-in after the GVAV goalkeeper spilled a Klaas Nuninga attempt. The game was an absolute battle and Cruyff had made it through.

The next week, Ajax would be hosting PSV at home. Cruyff was in the side again and he would light up the pitch. He also showed his desire to constantly make himself available for a pass from a team-mate and, when Ajax were out of possession, do what he could to stop a counter-attack; these would be the football foundations Cruyff would be commonly known for. He got himself another goal, this time showing the talent he had perfected in street football for dribbling at pace with the ball close to his feet before fooling the keeper with a cleverly disguised lob.

The game finished 5-0 and Cruyff had announced himself. After the game, Van der Veen was teary-eyed, overwhelmed by the realisation that the coaching and moulding of a kid he had first seen playing on the streets was about to pay dividends. Even he, though, could not have envisioned just how influential that kid would become.

* * *

Buckingham's second spell in the Dutch capital was not as successful as the first, largely due to sometimes being forced to use youth players because senior players left the club. This caused inconsistent results which could have ended in a relegation battle. After only six months, Ajax and Buckingham decided it was best for both parties that he move on and take the vacant role at English club Fulham. His successor at Ajax was Rinus Michels. One thing Buckingham did do in that six months was promote a certain Johan Cruyff into the first team. Legend has it that Buckingham had such an impact on the legend's life that Cruyff named him as the godfather to one of his children.

Buckingham's departure, opening the way for Michels to take over at Ajax, can be seen as the 'big bang moment' for the birth of Total Football and would help shape the team who would dominate Europe. Buckingham flirted with disaster for most of his three-year stint at Fulham, with players not showing the respect and desire his previous players gave him. Given that he had to contend with a tight budget and an eccentric chairman, it was a great accomplishment to avoid relegation in all three seasons. Some great stories have emerged from his time at Fulham and help to show what a character he was. If Fulham played badly on a Saturday, Buckingham would sometimes call a team meeting for the Sunday morning. He would enter the room without saying anything or allowing anyone to say anything before putting his coat and hat back on, walking out, climbing into his car and driving home. His squad would be suitably miffed given that he had just dragged them into work on what would usually be their day off.

Buckingham tried to introduce and implement a more universal system for Fulham to follow, a system like the one he helped create at Ajax. He wanted all Fulham's teams to play the same style, creating a clear pathway for homegrown and youth players to progress to the first team. Once again, English football proved it wasn't ready for him. He was replaced by another one of his protégés, a man who became one of the most successful and adored English managers ever – Bobby Robson.

After Buckingham had a stint in Greece, an unexpected call came from Catalonia. That game in the Inter-Cities Fairs Cup with Sheffield Wednesday had impressed FC Barcelona and they were calling for Buckingham to come and, as unlikely as it now sounds, help them avoid relegation. He did it, turning the campaign into a relative success and guiding the club to a fourth-place finish and European football. The following campaign (1970/71) was even more successful and followed a trend of Buckingham being especially successful in domestic cup competitions. Barcelona lifted the Copa del Rey, winning a great final 4-3 after extra time against a Valencia team who only beat Barcelona to the La Liga title on the head-to-head rule. The cup final was played in the Bernabeu, home of Barcelona's eternal rivals Real Madrid, and the trophy was handed over by a furious General Franco. Barcelona had given Buckingham the tools and trust to totally revamp the club. He was also effective in campaigning for the end of the Spanish FA's ban on signing foreign players, which would open the way for Cruyff's transfer to Barcelona in 1973. Cruyff would not be signing for Buckingham, however. The Englishman had to stand down in 1971 to receive treatment for a chronic back problem and was replaced by, you guessed it, Rinus Michels once again. Michels, as he did at Ajax, took the club to new heights with the help of Cruyff.

After undergoing surgery, Buckingham was out of the game until 1972, when he again ended up in Greece. He then had a spell at Sevilla, where he was handed a near-impossible task to avoid relegation from the top flight. With only 11 games left, including tricky fixtures against the division's top sides, he managed to delay the inevitable and it was only in the final game that Sevilla's fate was sealed. They had to play Barcelona in the penultimate game and then Real Madrid on the final day and Buckingham lost both games and his job. It was back to Greece and, after spells with Olympiacos and Rodos, his managerial career came to an end in the late 1970s.

Victor Frederick Buckingham passed away in 1995. His name does pop up in football discussions, but he is so often overlooked and ignored. He was mourned by the fans of Ajax and Barcelona as though he was a native, but he was born in Greenwich and died in Chichester, England. He paved the way for great managers who have taken the torch and passed it on to their successors. Sir Bobby Robson ignited many a successful career – none more so than his one-time translator, José Mourinho – and Cruyff created the famous 'Dream Team' when in charge of Barcelona and was succeeded by none other than Robson.

The other Total Football

While Ajax were leading a football revolution in the late 1960s and early 1970s, Valeriy Lobanovskyi, one of the most decorated managers of all time, was creating a coaching career at Dnipro Dnipropetrovsk in Ukraine which would earn him the job at Dynamo Kyiv in 1973. He is often credited with creating a similar side with Dynamo Kyiv as Michels did with Ajax and the Netherlands at a similar time. Lobanovskyi coached his team to follow the same principle of every player being able to switch to any other position on the field during a game. He claimed 33 official trophies in a management career stretching from 1969 to 2001 and is the only manager to win a major European trophy with an Eastern European club. At Kyiv, he was joined for a couple of years by his former team-mate Oleh Bazylevych, who acted as joint manager, and they pooled their expertise. Bazylevych was the theorist and Lobanovskyi was in charge of the training sessions and the coaching. Initially, their side were seen as a boring, unsporting side, as they made no attempt to conceal the fact they played for draws when away from home. It worked, though, and Kyiv won the league and cup. Going against every Total Football principle covered in this book so far, Lobanovskyi didn't stop there.

Although he was developing the same footballing ideas as Michels, Lobanovskyi placed huge emphasis on using scientific methods to enhance his side's performances. He used the scientist Anatoly Zelentsov to develop the ideal training plans for his players, based on mathematical calculations. Lobanovskyi would deny any links to Total Football, stating that he believed modern football was all about speed and power, although he did also stress that a player's technique had to be at the highest level. His football was built more on pressing the ball intensely, which was made possible by his players being in outstanding physical condition as a result of the rigorous, laboratory-designed training plans. Lobanovskyi coached technique and football philosophy to his players, too, but this was all geared towards the best ways to win football matches and based on statistics and data.

Players did rotate and were expected to be able to play in whatever area of the pitch they found themselves in, but Lobanovskyi's team was a machine built on science and aggressive front-foot defending. It was a fantastic, fascinating style that was clearly successful and has gone on to inspire football to become the science-driven, stat-hungry game it is today. It is a system and philosophy that has been recreated and tweaked many times since, bringing clubs success. However, it was never going to be the same as what Ajax were producing. In Italy, meanwhile, another team would come close to achieving Total Football, albeit they were a different story altogether.

During the mid-1970s, the armed and dangerous Lazio team fired their way to winning the scudetto, a miracle that was mainly down to their extremely intelligent coach Tommaso Maestrelli and his own version of Total Football. Maestrelli was born in Pisa in 1922. His father was an Italian State Railways employee, meaning the family moved around the country a lot before settling in Bari. This would be where he first signed for a professional football team. He played as a midfielder and his coach at Bari, the Hungarian Jósef Ging, gave Maestrelli his debut at the age of just 16. Maestrelli spent a decade with Bari before making an ill-fated move to Roma in 1948. This was the worst period in the history of AS Roma, ending in their only relegation.

Maestrelli avoided being relegated with AS Roma, as he was sold to Lucchese.

This would be his first taste of the dugout, as he covered the role of player-coach with Lucchese before moving back to Bari to end his playing career. He became the interim manager at Bari after being promoted from assistant following the departure of Pietro Magni. He didn't last long in charge of Bari, but he was granted another opportunity to showcase his coaching talents when AS Reggina (now Reggina 1914) hired him as their manager.

He did more than just showcase his talent; he wrote history, winning the club promotion to Serie B for the first time in 1965. The following year, Reggina almost pulled off a remarkable promotion to Serie A, but narrowly lost out to Lecco. Studying the results from his early years in management, it is clear that Maestrelli preferred front-foot attacking football. His pedigree in the lower leagues was undeniable at this point and, in 1968, he decided to move to Foggia in a bid to earn a place in Serie A. Also playing in Serie B at the time were Lazio, who were looking to win back their top-flight status. Maestrelli's first game at his future home, the Stadio Olimpico, was as Foggia manager and maybe this was when the Lazio board decided that he would one day be their man. The 1968/69 season was an experimental one for Maestrelli in which he first displayed his revolutionary and continental tactics. When Foggia faced Lazio on 29 December 1968, the Rome club were confident of a comfortable win.

The first half was fast-paced but was very much played in a typical Italian style, with both teams marking tightly. Despite a couple of penalty claims from Lazio, there was little between the sides at half-time. The second half was another story. Foggia came out flying and caught Lazio cold with a stunning counter-attack in what was a clear demonstration of the tactical nous Maestrelli would exhibit throughout his career. His teams would often go in at half-time, either behind or drawing, and then go on to win or, at worst, draw. Foggia found themselves with a surprise 1-0 lead at the Olimpico and, amazingly, they doubled their advantage. They would be pegged back by two late Lazio goals and, despite this scare against unfancied Foggia, the Rome club would go on to win the title and gain promotion back to Serie A.

After this first season of tampering and acclimatisation, Maestrelli would finally win promotion to Serie A as a coach, Foggia clinching the 1969/70 title by beating Livorno 3-1 on the final day. In the first half of the following season, Foggia were a revelation, lighting up Serie A with their impressive, attacking football. Maestrelli played with an ever-changing formation which was designed to get the best out of the players he had. Maestrelli was certainly one of the coaches who were close to cracking the Total Football code. He trained his squad so that they could all be attackers, sparing only the goalkeeper and two central defenders. Dutch scouts who were working on similar tactics in the early 1970s asked to watch some of his training sessions. If the draw in the Olimpico two years earlier made the Lazio chiefs sit up and take notice of Maestrelli, then the meeting of the two teams on 13 December 1970 made them draw up his contract. Playing at home this time, Foggia tore Lazio to shreds, winning 5-2. Unfortunately for Foggia, their results went downhill in the second half of the campaign and, despite only one home defeat all season, they were relegated on goal difference.

Lazio were also relegated that season and Maestrelli joined them that summer. Handed the task of gaining promotion back to Serie A, his first demand as manager was that the board did everything possible to keep striker Giorgio Chinaglia and defender Giuseppe 'Pino' Wilson at the club. Apart from his revolutionary tactical approach, what was also fascinating about Maestrelli was his taciturnity. In his book *Ultra*,[20] Tobias Jones describes how Maestrelli's character often disguised profound values. In his first speech as Lazio coach, he supposedly said to his players: 'I will speak little and that little will be seen to be a lot … We will love one another and avoid any misunderstanding. I consider loyalty the best gift given on this planet. We will grow together.' He was a mild-mannered person, a father figure to his squad and he would often invite his players to his home for meals. Chinaglia and Wilson had committed to staying and Maestrelli signed Luciano Re Cecconi from his former club Foggia. These three formed the spine of a team who would win promotion back to Serie A at the first time of asking.

In 1969, a bombing in Milan left 17 dead and more than 80 injured and further bombs were found in Milan's central train station and business quarters. In the capital, meanwhile, explosions also caused pandemonium. Italy was in the midst of what is now known as the 'Years of Lead', a name referring to the number of bullets that would riddle the country over the next decade. After the death of Benito Mussolini, Italy provided the USA with a perfect opportunity to build a relationship. The Americans were looking to forge relations with and capitalise on countries struggling within the shadow of the Iron Curtain. For Italians, this new relationship brought a surge in industrialisation and saw the country's economy grow at a rapid rate.

Cheap housing projects were built on the outskirts of the cities to house families who were looking for a better future. However, this growth was the spark that caused the 'Hot Autumn' of 1969. Trade unions obtained huge power across the country as workers demanded better working conditions and higher pay. Strikes and protest marches nearly brought the country to a standstill. Extreme left- and right-wing political groups saw an opportunity to influence the population by any means necessary and those from both sides with anarchistic tendencies looked to cause chaos and destruction.

These 'Years of Lead' would be the perfect era for Maestrelli's gun-toting, parachute-loving, self-declared fascist team. Lazio were armed and dangerous. Football was the only constant in a country in turmoil. There was a sense of relief every Sunday when it was game day. Considering Maestrelli's calm persona, it is astonishing just how much he achieved with a group of players who would make Wimbledon's 'Crazy Gang' look tame. They fought opposing teams on and off the field, most famously clashing with the Arsenal team outside a restaurant in Rome in 1970 after a European fixture. The Lazio players presented the Arsenal squad with leather purses and took great offence at the lack of gratitude shown. The Italians sparked a mass brawl that spilt out on to the street, leading to scenes Arsenal's Frank McLintock likened to 'something out of the Wild West'.

Maestrelli didn't just have to worry about the discipline of his players towards the opposition; they frequently fought amongst themselves. The players were so divided that different factions changed in separate dressing rooms and any infringement of one group's territory would often end in violence, as John Foot describes in his amazing book on the history of Italian football, *Calcio*. Training sessions would often include a practice game between the two dressing rooms and it is said that, on occasions, these games continued late into the night until one team won. Players were told to wear shin guards during these games and they all did, even those who didn't wear them for Serie A matches. Giorgio Chinaglia was often at the centre of the chaos. Chinaglia was born in Italy but raised in Wales after his father secured a job in the steel industry in Swansea.

A lot has been written about the man nicknamed 'Long John'. He had obvious talent on the pitch, boasting a big frame and a ferocious shot; his goals were at the centre of the success Lazio enjoyed. In 2000, he was voted Lazio's greatest-ever player. Thanks to his open admiration of right-wing politicians at the time, he didn't receive the same love from those with left-wing leanings.

However, it is likely he wasn't actually a fascist sympathiser – after all, one of his favourite pastimes was winding people up. On the pitch, he harassed opposing teams, screamed at referees, provoked the crowd and attacked his own players for not passing to him; he once ran after team-mate Vincenzo D'Amico and kicked him up the backside at the San Siro during one on-field dispute. Maestrelli was like a father to Chinaglia; the player would often stay at Maestrelli's house and would run over to the bench and embrace his manager whenever he scored.

Giuseppe 'Pino' Wilson, the rugged, often dirty defender who Maestrelli made his sweeper, was just as important as Chinaglia. He did not miss a single league game from 1971 to 1975 and, as captain, was the linchpin of the title-winning side in 1974. Wilson was actually born in Darlington, but was a lot less famous than the other 'Anglo-Italian', Chinaglia.

His parents met in Naples during the war and he was born in County Durham. However, the family moved back to Naples soon afterwards and Wilson never returned to the North East of England.

Perhaps the greatest student of Maestrelli's brand of football was the very blond, tall and gangly central midfielder, Luciano Re Cecconi, who flitted between the two Lazio dressing rooms. A real character in his own right, he was the only player who never carried a gun and he declared he knew nothing about politics. However, he was seen as a fascist, mainly due to his love of parachute-jumping, which was regarded in Italy at the time as a right-wing pastime.

On the pitch, he was the link between Pino's solid defending and Chinaglia's devastating finishing. He was brought to the club by Maestrelli from his old club, Foggia, for Lazio's first season back in Serie A.

In Maestrelli's version of Total Football, Re Cecconi was effectively played as the number four, the player in front of the defence, but his job was not just to win and retain the ball, but also to carry it forward, dragging his team up the pitch. Maestrelli played with two wingers – Pierpaolo Manservisi on the left and Luigi Martini on the right – who would also act as full-backs if needed. Maestrelli, though, wanted all his players to attack as much as possible. Mario Frustalupi would be the director in midfield, playing as Michels would want his number four to play, although Frustalupi would play higher and act as the final link to the attacking midfielder Franco Nanni.

This was a 5-3-2 formation which became a 3-3-4 when attacking, rather than the 4-3-3 associated with Total Football. In his first season in the top flight with Lazio, Maestrelli adjusted the midfield a lot from his promotion team, but what brought the most success was that he had built the best defence in the league. Only conceding 16 goals all season, the signing of Felice Pulici as goalkeeper helped this happen. Chinaglia was partnered up front by Renzo Garlaschelli in what would be a remarkable first season back in Serie A. Going into the final day, Lazio and Juventus were a point behind leaders AC Milan, who were beaten on the final day by Hellas Verona 5-3. Unfortunately for Lazio, they were also defeated, losing 1-0 to Napoli, and this handed the title to Juventus.

Nonetheless, it was a monumental achievement by Maestrelli's men, having just been promoted. The following season would provide an even bigger miracle.

Before home games, the Lazio squad used to stay at the L'Americana hotel, situated in the countryside around five miles outside Rome. 'The team would shoot at things all the time,' according to Franco Nanni. With real guns and real bullets, targets would include lamp-posts, birds, bins, each other and even, as John Foot recounts in *Calcio*,[20] a group of Roma fans who had gone to the hotel with the intention of keeping the Lazio players awake before a derby game. When flying to away games, the players would usually hand all their guns to the captain for safe-keeping. On one occasion, however, the pilot refused to take off until all the players had left their guns at the airport to be collected on their return. Defender Sergio Petrelli claims he once shot out a light in his hotel room because he couldn't be bothered to turn it off. Most of the protagonists now admit that their hobby did, at times, go too far, although they had great fun at the time. I'm guessing one unnamed player was on the end of a joke which ended in a shot being fired between his legs while he was in his hotel bed might not agree it was fun!

* * *

The 1973/74 season followed pretty much the same path as the campaign before. Lazio again boasted the best defence in the league and finished on the same number of points. However, their rivals fell away this time and Lazio were crowned champions. Maestrelli had completed his masterpiece. His ability to galvanise this bunch of maniacs, who hated one another and dressed in separate changing rooms, to come together every Sunday and conquer Serie A was remarkable. One game that underlined this was a home match against Verona. Lazio were losing 2-1 at half-time and, as they headed down the tunnel, Chinaglia was winding up for one of his famous rants. But the team were met by Maestrelli, who blocked the entrance to the changing rooms. Maestrelli simply said: 'Back on the field.' The players listened to their manager and headed straight back out and took up their positions. The crowd started going mad and, by the time Verona appeared more than ten minutes later, the Olimpico was a wall of sound. Lazio won the game 4-2.

It was fitting that Lazio were crowned champions on the penultimate day, at home against Foggia, a Chinaglia penalty hammered home like all the other 24 league goals he managed that campaign. The season's only blip came during their UEFA Cup game against Bobby Robson's Ipswich Town. Just as with the Arsenal game in 1970, it ended in a mass brawl. This time, however, the fighting broke out on the field and then spilt over into the dressing rooms. It was inexcusable violence in which, bizarrely, Chinaglia even ended up becoming the peacemaker. He was the only Lazio player Robson said could be excused, describing the rest of the squad as animals and savages. Robson said: 'If any of my players had acted even fractionally like that, they would never be allowed even to wear the shirt of Ipswich's youth team.'

Ipswich won the first leg in England 4-0. In the second leg, Lazio went 2-0 up after only half an hour but, in the 75th minute, Ipswich were given a dubious penalty and scored. At this point, the game turned sour. Objects were thrown on to the pitch by Lazio fans and these were then picked up by Lazio players and thrown at the Ipswich players. Lazio scored a further two goals but Ipswich then broke away to score their second and any hopes of a peaceful conclusion disappeared. At the final whistle, the Ipswich players ran for their dressing room, being kicked and punched by Lazio players as they went. Punches were thrown at the referee and the police guarded the Ipswich dressing room until it was safe to leave, an hour later.

With the club banned from the European Cup for the chaos in the Ipswich game, Maestrelli's focus was fully on defending their scudetto title in 1974/75. Lazio started fantastically and looked set to make it back-to-back titles. However, in March 1975, less than a year after winning the title, Maestrelli discovered that he had terminal stomach cancer. He immediately stepped down and was replaced by Roberto Lovati. The effect on the team was obvious and they lost 5-1 at home in the first game without Maestrelli. Lazio ended up slumping down to fourth place as Juventus won the league.

For a time, it seemed Maestrelli might recover, but when the 1975/76 season began, he was still hospitalised and tragically he died on 2 December 1976. Most of the best players were sold and Lazio finished fourth from bottom. Another tragedy would strike in January 1977. Re Cecconi, as mentioned earlier, loved to play pranks and jokes. Re Cecconi

and two friends, including Lazio player Piero Ghedin, w
shopping not far from the centre of Rome. While look
in a jewellery store, Re Cecconi, who had his hands in
pockets, thought it would be a good idea to jokingly she
'Stop, this is a robbery.' The shopkeeper, Bruno Tabocchi
had his back to the three men and instantly grabbed 1
shotgun. He pointed it at Ghedin, who instantly raised l
hands, and then at Re Cecconi, who did not. The jewell
shot him at close range. As he slumped to the ground, F
Cecconi muttered 'It's a joke, it's a joke.' Re Cecconi, who ha
a wife and two small children, died just 47 days after carryin
the coffin of Maestrelli, the man who transformed his caree
from his time at Foggia, making him a champion.[20]

Maestrelli's success was down to his fabulously attacking,
almost Total Football style of play. He shared the beliefs of
the great Rinus Michels and those who have followed him
– the likes of Johan Cruyff, Pep Guardiola and Louis van
Gaal. They have all created superb teams, winning trophies,
breaking records and producing wonderful players who
symbolised their sides. What makes Maestrelli different,
however, is that the others used Total Football and its
theories as the core of their teams. Players who didn't fit the
style were not included, no matter their talent. Players with
the wrong attitude were also cast aside. Maestrelli never had
this luxury and he used his exceptional man-management
skills to nurture his crazy players to not only perform at
their best but to carry out the most physically demanding
and mentally challenging brand of football. This makes
him more comparable to Vic Buckingham than other Total
Football pioneers.

The success of his Lazio side was, of course, down to
his players and their performances, but I think you can

confidently say that, without Maestrelli at the helm, there
is no way they would have won the scudetto. They may have
ended up trapped in Serie B for several years. This is backed
up by their dramatic slump once Maestrelli's illness forced
him away from the dugout. Who knows what else Maestrelli
could have achieved for the game if he had not so tragically
passed away? He should never be forgotten for what he did
manage. Bringing success to every team he coached, working
his way up through the leagues and winning them all along
the way. A fantastic manager, coach and friend to his players.
A legend.

At this point, it feels as if the time was ripe, with all
that had come before – from Scotland and Hungary to 'La
Maquina' and the 'Golden Team' – for the 1970s to produce
something special and there are theories as to why it was
Amsterdam that ended up being the birthplace of Total
Football. The dynamic behind Maestrelli's Lazio success
was so different in many ways to the Total Football being
created in Amsterdam. Lazio were the complete opposite of
the 'family' Ajax created.

Ajax, in the 1960s, became many Amsterdammers'
family. They became known as a Jewish club, but this was
only because, when investors began to put their money into
the club, some of these were Jewish businessmen. Football
clubs were seen as a bad investment in those days and not
many businesses or banks would choose to invest in them,
but Ajax was different. By buying into the club, you became
part of a family and this was the perfect setting for those
without a family, which, after the Holocaust, was the case
for so many Jews residing in Amsterdam. Ajax became a club
at which many Jewish business owners mingled. Leo Horn,
who owned a textile business, was one of them. During

the Second World War, he was part of the Amsterdam Resistance and, using the name Dr Van Dongen, he and a group of ten men managed to save the lives of many Jews. Following the war, he became a football referee and he was in charge when Hungary famously demolished England 6-3 at Wembley in 1953. These Jewish businessmen would often hire Ajax players to work for their companies. Cruyff worked for Harry Blitz and Piet Keizer worked for Horn and Ruud Krol sewed for George Horn. Ruud Krol's father was named Kuki and was an integral part of Horn's Resistance team, helping hide George Horn and many other Jews from the Nazis.[17]

Although not Jewish, Cruyff shared a sense of loss with the Jews involved in Ajax, as he had also lost a close family member. It is remarkable how Amsterdam, a city so devastated by the war, emerged from it with this aspect of togetherness and family and how football played a major part in that. Simon Kuper explains in *Ajax, The Dutch, The War* how the war impacted the feelings and the needs of the city's football fans. In Britain, football was – and still is – seen as a kind of war. Players go into battle and fight for the right to win. By the 1970s, the Dutch had rid themselves of this culture, helped by the style of football being created.

Post-war Amsterdam was regarded as an incredibly dull place, far removed from the impressive, progressive city it is now. Just as had happened in Vienna in the early 1900s, a new style of football promoted and expressed the feelings of the city it was being created in. Ajax had the perfect concoction to create a footballing ideal. The society in Amsterdam was leaning towards the bourgeois of Vienna earlier in the century, which created 'Scheiberspiel', and, after years of nurturing and coaching, Ajax boasted some of the greatest footballers ever. All the club needed now was a top team to play against to showcase it all. Obviously, Ajax couldn't play the English national team, so they had to settle for the next best thing at the time, Liverpool FC.

* * *

When Rinus Michels took over from Vic Buckingham at Ajax for the remainder of the 1964/65 season, steering them clear of relegation, Cruyff was used sparingly in the first team. He made only five appearances in the remainder of that season and, although his performances were praised in the club's official match reports, his outstanding talent came with some concerns. He was skinny, had a temper he often couldn't control and was still underweight. In his early appearances, Cruyff would never take corners because he couldn't reach the box with his flag kicks. This was amplified by a toe injury that he sustained and ignored; it got worse and the swelling became so bad that his foot wouldn't fit into any football boot available on the market. Michels knew someone in Haarlem who could help and bespoke boots were made for Cruyff. They were ankle height and weighed a ton because of the lead tips inserted to protect his swollen little toe.

By the summer of 1965, when Cruyff was 18, he was offered a new contract at Ajax and was fuming with it, tearing it up in the boardroom after being offered less money than the rest of the squad. As Cruyff grew up around the club and knew almost everyone involved in it, he was confident enough to threaten to leave. Most of the other players would be represented by their fathers or a club donor who had got them into the club. Cruyff had no one. His mother was too friendly with the board members and would side with them.

Cruyff got his new contract, on his terms, and helped secure deals for a number of other first-team players. Cruyff was now one of the first crop of professional footballers in Dutch football and no longer had to work for Harry Blitz. In turn, Cruyff now had to train more than the non-professionals and Michels would prove to be the most important father figure of them all for Cruyff, allowing him to grow into what he became.

From the start, Michels never pandered to Cruyff. As a player, Michels had been regarded as rather lazy but was friendly and a great team-mate. Now he was to be addressed as Mr Michels and he kept a distance between himself and his players. The players had to understand that what he wanted for them was not to have fun but to carry out the specific tasks he assigned to them for the good of the team. Michels's traits were unusual for a manager at that time. The well-educated Michels would spend time teaching his players in a classroom-type setting and was able to easily break down team tactics and his analysis of opponents. He drew from his experience as a teacher at a school for deaf children. He created an environment for Cruyff which consisted of clarity and structure with methodical patterns. Cruyff loved the tactical and technical aspects but, when it came to cross-country running or fitness work, Cruyff was not so keen. Michels, though, would offer no easy ride for his soon-to-be talisman. Michels once punished Cruyff for cheating in a running drill by ordering him to come in on a day off for an extra session.

This time it would involve rowing at Bosbaan Lake at 8am. Cruyff, waiting by the lake in the cold, was greeted by Michels, who was in his car, still wearing his pyjamas. He wound down the window and told Cruyff it was far too early for him and he was going back to bed, leaving the player alone by the lake. It was a ploy straight from the Vic Buckingham playbook but it didn't really work and Cruyff continued to take liberties in training sessions. At the start of the season, Cruyff was asked to mature in the second team. On 24 October 1965, he got a chance to play in the first team and would end up earning a spot in the first team on a rotating basis. It was decided that he would play in the first team on alternate weeks. His brilliance would still be accompanied by petulance and the newspapers' praise for his play was always accompanied by criticism of his attitude and arrogance. He would kick players after losing the ball.

What fans quickly picked up on, though, was his ability to find space. In that space, he was able to flourish and cause damage to the opposition. If he found a pocket of space and did not receive the ball, he was not slow to admonish his team-mates. Although still only 18, he would bark out instructions, letting them know they had a lot to learn until they understood the game as much as he did. Most of this behaviour came in the games for the second team, but Cruyff was making a name for himself, appearing in magazines and newspapers.

The rest of the first team were becoming the cohesive, rule-abiding players that taskmaster Michels wanted them to be. Michels was beginning to open up about the type of football he wanted his team to play and that would be focusing on a team with defenders who could attack and attackers who could defend, players on the move all the time and being able to slot into any area of the pitch for the good of the team. This was Total Football he was talking about. Michels's vision was progressing but Cruyff was becoming a headache. His talent was needed but there was a general consensus that his problem was that he believed he was the only person in the world who fully understood football.

Cruyff also suffered from chronic migraines; it had been a problem throughout his teenage years, but they were now getting worse. Michels, despite having disciplinary problems with Cruyff, still knew he needed him. Amazingly, he would turn to science to find a solution. He suggested the board hire a psychologist to assess Cruyff, partly to help with his migraines but also to learn how the club could best deal with his attitude. In early January 1966, Cruyff met with psychologist Jan Silkboer, who concluded that his aggression was an overcompensation for a feeling of inferiority and insecurity.[18] The assessment was that, while Cruyff was undoubtedly a great footballer, he only enjoyed the game because it gave him the opportunity to achieve something for himself. Not only that, but Silkboer believed there was little-to-no sign of a bond with Ajax and that Cruyff wanted to sell himself to the highest bidder.

The Ajax board were already conscious they needed to handle Cruyff with great delicacy, which is why he was rotated between the first and second teams to avoid burning him out. The psychologist's report backed this up and would most likely have confirmed underlying issues Michels was perhaps already aware of. Matters would be taken out of Michels's hands, though. He needed Cruyff to play on 9 January against Feyenoord. Ajax were six points behind Feyenoord and he knew they had to be at their best in the fierce atmosphere at De Kuip. Injuries meant Cruyff would play from the start.

It is amazing how things just click into place at this point. Cruyff needed discipline from Michels and the feeling of belonging to a team structure to unlock his full potential while Michels needed Cruyff as the last piece of his Total Football puzzle. Cruyff was sensational that day, untouchable as he danced around the pitch. Relentless in the forward line, he popped up all over. Defenders were cautious of him even when he didn't have the ball, as he was sharp and ready to pounce on any loose balls or poor touches. Ajax went 1-0 down, but the equalising goal showed the telepathic relationship Cruyff had with Keizer as they combined in a move which Cruyff finished off.

Ajax didn't manage a win – the game ended 1-1 – but Cruyff had cut the ropes that were holding him back. Without him, Ajax were a slow, sluggish side who laboured their way to results. With him, they were fast and dynamic and their attacking style would flourish. By March 1966, Cruyff had become a regular in the starting XI, never being dropped again. The negative reports on Cruyff were also a thing of the past. During the second part of the season, his attitude seemed to differ. He was now part of the team. It would seem that the psychologist's visit had worked wonders and, although the results may have been damning, it appeared Cruyff was now realising that both he and his team could perhaps benefit from the character traits highlighted by the report.

* * *

On 15 May 1966, Ajax were sitting at the top of the table and, after a comfortable win over FC Twente, they were crowned champions. Cruyff was described as having been the best player in the league that season by a distance and, despite only fully establishing himself in the team midway through the campaign, he managed to finish as the club's top scorer with 25 goals in 19 matches. He was also now boasting some muscles in the stick-thin legs and had grown several inches. All of sudden, all the concerns around him being too weak, too small and having a terrible attitude had vanished.

Michels was now almost fully content he had all the components and players to create the perfect style and a team to conquer club football. As Ajax grew even more professional, they signed Velibor Vasović in the summer of 1966. He was a tough central defender who was aged 26 and had plenty of experience. He was signed to take Ajax to the next level and, for Cruyff, this was brilliant, as his ambitions to express his talents could only be contained in the Netherlands for a short period; he wanted to showcase his ability to the world and the European Cup was the perfect stage.

Michels began pre-season in the same manner as the previous one. The team would be going into their second full year together and he was making sure they were programmed to perform his tasks; you could say he was building a machine. Unlike the machine built at River Plate, this one was connected with a social uprising which would only enhance its impact on society.

Amsterdam was now the unofficial hippy capital of Europe and, although this was a million miles away from the authoritarian characteristics of Michels, Total Football was built around space and space means freedom. The players of Ajax now knew their jobs and, while the strict objectives set by Michels did not sound like they would go hand in hand with freedom, somehow they did in this Ajax team. Just as in the Hungarian 'Golden Team', players interchanged and the 4-2-4 formation was utilised by Michels. By December 1966, Ajax were at the top of the league. After 14 games played they had scored 57 goals. The front four of Swart,

Cruyff, Nuninga and Keizer were tearing up the league and making all the sporting headlines. Their next game would be in the European Cup against Liverpool, champions of a country basking in the success of having won the World Cup for the first time that summer.

As Bill Shankly prepared his side for the first leg in Amsterdam on 7 December 1966, he was asked about Ajax and quipped: 'That's a cleaning fluid.' He would come to rue under-estimating Liverpool's opponents. On the day of the match, Swart gave Cruyff and Barry Hulshoff a lift to the stadium, but he had trouble starting his car. They had to take turns pushing the car until it started and they arrived at the stadium late and knackered. However, like the car's ignition, Ajax would spark into life that night. Thick fog had descended over the Dutch capital and, although it would impact the scoreline, I doubt it had much to do with the result. The misty conditions would only serve to prove just how cohesive this Ajax team now were. Swart claimed that the players couldn't even see the ball at times, that they could only hear it, but Michels had his players so well drilled that one player's movement would trigger a team-mate to move into another position.

This was Total Football. It was here, although you could hardly see it through the fog. Ajax won 5-1. Keizer was missing due to injury and Michels had to use Cees de Wolf up front, but the performance showed how capable this team were, even without key players. Ajax were 3-0 up at half-time and, after a half of dominance and fluid football from the Dutch team, Liverpool had to come out and attack them in the second period. Liverpool had a lot of the ball, but Ajax defended well and scored another couple on the counter-attack. Liverpool missed a number of chances, but

Ajax deserved to win comfortably and they did. Shankly told the press that the fog had played a major part in the result and claimed that Ajax had played a defensive game, preventing Liverpool from finding any rhythm. This was, of course, a smokescreen in itself. Shankly predicted Liverpool would win 7-0 in the return leg and go through.

In fact, the return leg, in which Ajax welcomed back Keizer, finished 2-2 with two goals from Cruyff which he would later refer to as two of the best he ever scored. Shankly went into the away dressing room after the game to congratulate his opponents on a fantastic performance. It was a good job the Scot wasn't there when Cruyff and his team-mates headed for the showers chanting 'Shankly better pack his bags, hi-ha-ho!' to the tune of a famous nursery rhyme. [18]

The Ajax team had now earned recognition across the continent, but the European Cup dream didn't last long; they lost in the next round against Dukla Prague. The setback would prompt Michels to look at his defensive structure. This is when Vasović became a regular. His impact on the team would be similar to that which Mandi had at MTK. Vasović was given the role of aggressive defender but he was also the base from which Ajax built their attacks. Between 1967 and 1970, Ajax monopolized the league title and, in 1969, were runners-up in the European Cup. The years 1970–73 were perhaps when the system built by Michels produced its most entertaining and successful football. Total Football had been created, but the formations and the players in the squad had not yet been finalised. On paper, Michels was, by 1970, deploying a 4-3-3 formation.

But it is pointless to label this side with a set formation, as the team were built to be fluid and attack space whilst pressing the ball intensely. Using 4-3-3 as a starting point allowed more space for the interchanging of positions. These switches would usually take place via overlaps or would happen down one side of the pitch and sometimes through the middle. On the left-hand side, Ajax would have Ruud Krol, Gerrie Mühren and Keizer. Wim Suurbier, Arie Haan and Sjaak Swart were on the right. The centre-half position was filled by Vasović and, later, Horst Blankenburg or Barry Hulshoff. The centre-half would interchange with Neeskens and Cruyff down the middle. Neeskens was a vital part of the system, as his pressing was the starting point for most of Ajax's play. As a midfielder, he would often fly into the opponents' area of the pitch and hunt down the ball. This gave Cruyff the space to retreat from the forward line into deeper positions, popping up all over the pitch to suit what the team needed at any given time.

The system worked almost automatically and replacements slotted in unnoticed when first-choice players were missing. Ajax won three back-to-back European Cups in the years 1971–73, but it was Ştefan Kovács who led them to the last two after Michels left for Barcelona. This demonstrated how well the system Michels put in place worked. Ajax continued to dominate Europe even after he left and it was the legacy of his beliefs, supplemented by a golden generation of players, that allowed Kovács to take a back seat and still succeed. Kovács made slight tactical tweaks but he let his assistant, Bobby Haarms, organise training and the day-to-day stuff while Cruyff and Keizer were given extra power over the team.

* * *

In his book *Brilliant Orange*, David Winner captures the genius of Dutch football much better than I ever could. For those playing Total Football at the time, it wasn't ever really addressed as a concept. Swart was once quoted as saying that the term Total Football came from the English, that the Dutch never actually had a name for it. Winner argues the style of play was influenced by the social climate in the Netherlands at the time, growing alongside arts and culture. He also stresses that, although enjoyed by many, Total Football is still only one approach to a game which has many fascinating and exciting styles.

The Mühren brothers, Gerrie and Arnold, played at different times but their careers captured what it was like to play Total Football in the period when it was being created. It had an impact on them and they, in turn, impacted other teams who were not immersed in the ideology of Total Football.

Arnold, the younger of the brothers by five years, was a key player in Bobby Robson's Ipswich Town team as they won the 1981 UEFA Cup and narrowly missed out on the First Division title, finishing as runners-up in 1981 and 1982. Arnold was then transferred to Manchester United, helping them win the 1983 FA Cup and becoming a cult hero at Old Trafford. He was also one of the few players outside the UK and Ireland who were playing in England in the late 1970s and early 1980s.

Gerrie broke through into the Ajax set-up before his brother and kept him out of the team. Also a left-footer, he was a real artist on the pitch and his football travels took him to Spain.

* * *

In Seville, Gerrie was at Real Betis when they won the Copa del Rey in 1977 but was denied a winner's medal because foreigners were not allowed to play in the competition then. He was, however, named as Spain's player of the year and became a club legend during his three years with Betis.

Like many of the Dutch greats, the Mühren brothers learnt their trade on the streets, not far from Amsterdam (approximately 18km) in the small village of Volendam, a different world entirely from the capital. The beautiful Volendam, popular with tourists for its picturesque dwellings, is the Netherlands' most famous fishing village. In the early part of the 20th century, numerous artists – including Picasso and Renoir – would use the village as a retreat. What is truly remarkable, though, is the number of talented individuals who have emerged from such a small place. The pop groups Band Zonder Naam (Band Without A Name) and The Cats both come from Volendam. The Cats made noise all over the world from the 1960s to the 1980s and BZN, although having limited international success, are huge in the Netherlands.

Living up to the British stereotype, everyone in Volendam seems to be related in some way. The founder and leading member of The Cats was another Arnold Mühren and was the footballing brothers' cousin. Jan and Pé Mühren were twins in a family of 12. Jan was the father of the footballers while Pé became a writer. BZN also helped produce another household name in Holland – Jan Smit, a singer-turned-TV presenter.

In 2013, Smit joined the board of the village's professional football team, FC Volendam, whose stadium announcer was once Pé Mühren and he now has a stand named after him.

Although Volendam is situated just outside Amsterdam, its inhabitants have a very Latin feel to them and the village

THE BIRTH OF TOTAL FOOTBALL

is one of the only places in Holland that is 100 per cent Catholic. It is said that during a war between the Netherlands and Spain hundreds of years ago, it was the Basques who created Volendam, transforming it from a tiny harbour that served neighbouring Edam into the vibrant, tight-knit community it is now, and leaving behind some of their Latin origins and beliefs. This maybe helps explain why this village has generated so many great talents.

I am going to start with Gerrie, not just because he is the older brother, but because, having never played in England, his name is sometimes overlooked when remembering the great Dutch players of the 1970s. The brothers both learnt their skills on the streets of their beloved Volendam and, as they played together all the time, Gerrie taught his younger brother a trick or two. Gerrie started his career at Volendam and, in 1968, he moved to Ajax, spending eight years in Amsterdam, a period which saw him win pretty every trophy available at club level. Gerrie's early career at Ajax was under the guidance of Rinus Michels but when Kovács came in and handed more power to Cruyff and Keizer, they knew Gerrie's qualities. It was Gerrie who was given the duty of slotting away penalties. The Dutch are famously poor at spot kicks, but Gerrie was a master.

Despite all their trophies, the most cherished moment for this great Ajax team actually came in a European Cup semi-final against Real Madrid in April 1973. Ajax travelled to Spain for the second leg with a 2-1 lead from the first game in Amsterdam.

After that game in Madrid, the Mühren brothers walked away from the stadium together, surrounded by Madrid fans, who were discussing with great excitement what they had just seen. A group of fans, mistakenly thinking the Mührens were

Ajax supporters, approached them and started mimicking Gerrie's ball-juggling motion. Arnold pointed at his brother and told them: 'This is the guy who did the juggling.' They didn't believe him, though, as they couldn't imagine that a superstar footballer would be walking the streets among the fans. Gerrie's beliefs surrounding his celebrity status were very egalitarian and deeply Dutch. 'A doctor came to me to ask for my autograph and I asked him for his autograph instead. It is only luck that we could play soccer. We could not see how good we were. We needed the crowd, the crowd needed us,' he said. 'It's better to be modest. In Holland, they are a little bit cool and I prefer that. No one here has ever asked for my autograph. I am one of them. In Volendam, it is normal; everyone lives normal lives.'

* * *

At the start of the 1974/75 season, it was looking more likely that Cruyff would eventually join his old mentor Michels in Catalonia. After Ajax claimed their third consecutive European Cup in 1973, Kovács left and was replaced by George Knobel. The new coach got off to a terrible start. Deciding to take Kovács' back-seat approach to new levels, he asked the squad to anonymously vote for who they wanted to be the captain for the upcoming season. Knobel would later say he believed he was only following an established club tradition because Haarms had informed him that was how it was always done. The vote caused great divides in an already tired group. Cruyff lost his captaincy, receiving somewhere between three and seven votes (the results have never been disclosed), and the squad was slowly dissolving. Cruyff left for Barcelona, igniting a mass exodus. Gerrie Mühren signed for Real Betis.

Gerrie was once dubbed the 'forgotten football hero' of Dutch football. In the city of Seville, however, the humble Dutchman is far from forgotten. 'In Seville, they treat me like a king. I don't like it. It's better to be modest.' Gerrie and his family loved their time in Seville and his wife, Grietje, talked about the similarities to Volendam, saying: 'The people are hospitable, just like in Volendam. When people meet outside on the street, we would have dinner with them in the evening or they would come to us.'

When Gerrie arrived at Real Betis in 1976, the Hungarian manager Ferenc Szusza was his new coach and the club had put together one of the greatest squads in their history. Legendary forward Rafael Gordillo also joined the squad that season, earning promotion from the B team, and Real Betis would go on to win the Copa del Rey. Although Gerrie sat out that success due to the Spanish rules on foreign players, his classy performances were rewarded by the federation with the Spanish footballer of the year award. This was his most cherished award and sat in prime position in his living room back in Volendam once he retired. He won this award at a time when his old friends Johan Cruyff and Johan Neeskens were at Barcelona and another Netherlands star, Johnny Rep, was at Valencia.

In his first game for Real Betis, Gerrie faced city rivals Sevilla and he would win over the whole fanbase in the most bizarre but most Mühren way possible. The fans knew all about his footballing talents but, after watching a shocking team performance and a defeat at the hands of their fierce rivals, the Betis fans were furious. At full time, several hundred gathered outside the stadium to vent their displeasure. The players and staff were diverted to a back exit where they knew they wouldn't run into any of the furious supporters. Gerrie walked straight out of the front door. At first, there was silence; then the fans broke into applause and Gerrie was dubbed 'hombre de cojones', which translates as 'man with balls'. In his first season, he played fantastically as a midfielder, just like he did at Ajax, mainly operating on the left. He spent three seasons at Betis and, towards the end of this stint, started to play more as a defensive midfielder and was given a free role which allowed him to receive the ball in deep positions and start attacks from there. Betis fans are known for being quite aggressive but Mühren certainly won them over and will always be remembered as one of their true greats.

Gerrie was given the perfect goodbye gift from Betis when, in the summer of 1979, it was announced that he would be returning home. The club organised a friendly match with FC Volendam to wave goodbye to their hero. In the first half, Gerrie played for Real Betis but then swapped the green and white jersey for the orange of FC Volendam for the second half. The fans in the crowd were brought to tears; they just weren't ready to see him leave. Gerrie had spent ten years at the top of the European game from making his debut for Ajax in 1968 to his transfer back to where it all started for him in 1979. He spent a season back at Volendam before moving to MVV Maastricht for a season in 1980/81. Seiko SA were the best team in Hong Kong in the 1980s and Gerrie added two league titles to his honours in the two seasons he played for them in 1981/82.

He returned to Holland with Football Club Dordrecht (DS '79) in 1982 and in the two seasons he spent with them, he won promotion before being relegated back down to the Eerste Divisie the following season. Gerrie had one last stint at his beloved Volendam before, in 1985, he called time on his career, a fantastic one which does not get the widespread respect it deserved. His ten years at Ajax and Real Betis should have been enough to cement his place in football's history books forever, but maybe it is his lack of presence in the Dutch national squad which prevents his name from being mentioned alongside the world's greatest players.

He had a chance to announce his presence to the world in 1974, when Michels took the Netherlands so close to winning the World Cup. Gerrie would have been one of the guaranteed starters in that squad and he was called up, but he put his family first and decided not to go to the tournament because his son was ill. Despite his wife urging him to play, he decided against it and stayed in Volendam that summer. He made ten appearances for his country leading up to that tournament but would never be capped again.

After retiring, Gerrie was never far from the game. He had a scouting job with Ajax and he and brother Arnold, with financial support from Reebok, travelled around the Netherlands coaching. They visited around 150 amateur clubs, teaching basic technique and passing skills. This sums up how Gerrie approached the game; to him, it wasn't just a spectacle but mainly a strategic game that players must enjoy just as much as the spectators. 'I didn't like the crowd making a noise. You have to be able to listen. Atmosphere is good but if there was a noise near me, I would move to the other side of the stadium. I want to hear the game, the players, the ball.'

Sadly, on 19 September 2013, Gerrie Mühren passed away. He died of myelodysplastic syndrome (MDS) in his home town of Volendam. His legacy will live on forever, especially in the hearts of Ajax and Real Betis fans. Despite the 'forgotten hero' tag, he did have admirers from all over the world. In Jamaica, at a museum near Bob Marley's grave, is a book which includes the names of people the reggae legend admired, Gerrie Mühren is included. When Gerrie discovered this, it made him extremely happy.

The Mühren brothers both forged their own great legacies in the game, but their core beliefs and talents were much the same. Gerrie, as the older brother, laid the base on the streets of Volendam, where the brothers first played together, and they were together at Ajax in the 1970s. When the Ajax team was dismantled and Gerrie headed for Spain, Arnold stayed in Amsterdam, displaying similar modesty to his brother and an equally magical left foot, and paved his own way towards spreading the Mühren name across the continent.

'My brother played with his friends. When I was five or six, I started joining in,' Arnold recalls in *Brilliant Orange*. 'We weren't exceptional. Everybody could play to a high standard. If you couldn't play football, bad luck – you had to go in goal.' Arnold also says that playing with a tennis ball most of the time is what gave him and his brother such great technique – similar to the stories of Cruyff's childhood. Playing on the road meant Gerrie and Arnold learned to keep their balance to avoid falling on the hard ground and the speed at which the games were played helped their technique under pressure. 'No one ever told us how to play. It was all natural. When we joined Volendam when we were 12, we already knew how to play.' Arnold's attitude, along with this experience of round-the-clock street football, allowed him to become the perfect professional.

He met his wife when he was 19 and never took his eye off becoming the best player he could be. 'I was only interested in football. I lived like a monk! No smoking, no drinking, go to bed early. People say I didn't have a youth, but I've had the best life.' Arnold, despite his professional approach, maintained that his core reason for playing football was that he enjoyed it. 'It started off as a hobby, to take part with a group of players. When I ended my career, it was still a hobby – a well-paid hobby. You have to see it as a hobby.'

After graduating from Volendam's academy, Arnold followed in his brother's footsteps by heading to Ajax. Arnold, who was still only 20 when he moved, didn't make that many appearances, with his older brother the preferred choice. Arnold, explaining the modesty he and his brother shared, once said: 'It's in our character, putting yourself in the service of others. Football is a team sport in which you have to use each other's qualities. We were at the service of the better players.' This quote shows the professionalism and determination Arnold had, something his team-mates would take note of, most importantly Cruyff, who would eventually end up calling on Arnold's services 12 years after the two played together.

Despite his bit-part role, Arnold still managed to pick up some silverware in his first two seasons at Ajax. He won two league titles and the KNVB Cup and was involved in the last of Ajax's European Cup triumphs, starting the famous semi-final second leg at the Bernabeu. When the team was broken up the season after this third European title, Arnold was one of the few who stayed. He got more game time in the 1973/74 season before heading for FC Twente in the summer of 1974.

At the opposite end of the country to Amsterdam and Volendam is the city of Enschede. This would be Arnold's new stomping ground, spending four years at FC Twente, helping the club to the final of the UEFA Cup in 1975, where they lost to Borussia Mönchengladbach. Coached by Hennes Weisweiler, the West German club were one of the first teams really inspired by Ajax and their attacking football and Mönchengladbach dominated domestic football for a period in the 1970s. Mühren would also add another KNVB Cup to his trophy cabinet when FC Twente won the competition in 1977. Now that he was playing a more prominent role in the team compared to his role at Ajax, he was starting to get the recognition his talents deserved.

However, his relationship with the management deteriorated at the end of the 1977/78 season and Arnold hoped for move back to his home FC Volendam. A lack of funds prevented this and he was spending the summer back at his home in Volendam contemplating his next move when there was a knock on his front door.

His performances for Twente had caught the eye of Ipswich Town manager Bobby Robson, so much so that, hearing he might be available after falling out with Twente, Robson got on the next flight to Amsterdam and headed for Volendam. Robson turned up at the door of the Mührens' home in Volendam with the hope of persuading Arnold to join Ipswich and, after he left, Arnold and his wife researched every little thing about the club and the area of Suffolk. Arnold knew it would be a huge risk to play in England, but he also appreciated it was a chance to advance his career.

The next day, Arnold and his wife, Gerrie, boarded a private plane hired by Robson to take them to Ipswich. A final touch was organised by Robson. As the jet flew over Portman Road and the adjacent training pitches, a training session was being held and all the players and staff looked up and waved. Upon landing, the Mührens were welcomed by a swarm of fans chanting Arnold's name. The wily Robson was trying all the tricks he knew but, when Arnold left to return home without agreeing to sign, Robson thought he had missed his chance. However, Arnold had been won over by Robson's approach and personality during the visit. He called as soon as he got home to confirm that he would sign.

Robson had been at Ipswich for nine years before he signed Mühren, during which time he had established them as a top six side in England's top flight. However, despite winning the 1978 FA Cup, Robson's team needed some fresh blood and £150,000, a pretty hefty sum of money back in 1978, is what it took for Ipswich to land Mühren. The following February, Ipswich went out and bought Frans Thijssen, a team-mate of Arnold's at Twente. The duo formed a 'semi-wide midfield' partnership. Anyone who is familiar with the term 'half space' will know the areas in which these two operated at a time well before the term became famous. These two would ensure that Ipswich stayed away from the long ball style of play and their newly mastered fluid football would send them flying up the league table.

As is always the case with foreign imports to the English game, the first question was 'will they handle it?', a question asked as if the game in England is far superior to anywhere else in the world. Well, Arnold answered that question in the best way possible. Instead, he would ask whether England could handle him? Rather than him adapting to the English game, he made the English game adapt to him.

He had the perfect manager to help him achieve this. Robson was not known for his tactical approach, but what made him one of the best was his second-to-none man-management and his ability to develop new players, his enthusiastic manner bringing the best out of his charges. Speaking to David Winner for *Brilliant Orange*, Arnold talked about his debut for Ipswich. He remembered it was against Liverpool and that he was up against England international Terry McDermott. 'He was a very good runner and we ran up and down the wing all day. Neither of us touched the ball because it kept going over our heads.' This was a major culture shock for Arnold, who was now noticing the differences in the football he was used to in his home nation.

After the game, Mühren went straight to see his manager and told Robson: 'It's better to put the linesman in instead of me. He can run up and down all day, too. If you want to get the best out of me, you have to give me the ball. That's what I need. That's why you bought me.' We have talked about Mühren's humble nature, but this act on his debut for a team who were all British and had played in the same way for years, shows that Arnold also knew when to become the leader. This was not for his own personal gain; he didn't want to be the star player, he just wanted to get the most out of his team-mates and that is exactly what he did. Ipswich learned to feed Arnold the ball and when Frans Thijssen arrived, the two Dutchmen gave Ipswich another dimension. Their vision and skill would bring poise and intelligence to the team. Arnold, though, also admired the English players. 'They have things I didn't have. So strong in the air, strong tacklers. They can run all day. If you could put Dennis Bergkamp's skills with Tony Adams's strength and spirit, you would have the complete player.'

In the 13 years in which Robson was Ipswich manager, he only signed 18 players from other clubs, largely relying on promoting players through the ranks from the club's well-stocked academy. One of these youth players ended up being my Sunday league team's manager. He made the trip from

Newcastle to Suffolk as a schoolboy and tells some great tales of his time at the club. Kevin Dodds, a left-back looking to take the place of legendary full-back Mick Mills, was part of the Ipswich set-up for around 18 months and can vouch for the tales of Robson's great nature and how it was Robson's belief in making all players as equal as possible that helped create the atmosphere that would bring the club so much success. Kevin recalls many a training session or matchday when members of the first team would stay behind to watch the youngsters and give them tips. Kevin remembers Mühren being one of these players. Even if the tips weren't always technical pointers, Arnold and his team-mates would offer attitude and lifestyle advice on how to make sure they landed a professional contract. Arnold was the best man to advise on professionalism as, even by the time he reached England, he still hadn't changed his ways; it was still no drinking and having early nights.

'Mühren was a wonderful passer, great vision. I cannot think of anyone I would rate higher as a professional than Arnold. No one works harder and when the match is over, he won't go out drinking. He goes to bed.' To have this said about you by anyone would be enough to make you happy. These were the words of Bobby Robson, though, so they carry a lot more meaning and help show just what an impact Arnold had on the Ipswich team. The first season with Ipswich was slightly stop-start, but that is understandable considering Mühren and Thijssen were still settling and making their mark. The 1980/81 season is remembered by Ipswich fans as one of the best in the club's history. They came close to emulating Alf Ramsey's 1962 champions, narrowly losing out to Aston Villa in the First Division title race. But it was their performance in the UEFA Cup that wrote the team into the history books. They beat Dutch side AZ Alkmaar 5-4 on aggregate in the final and Arnold Mühren added the UEFA Cup to the European Cup he won with Ajax.

In his final season at Ipswich, the club would again be pushing for the title and would again come up just short, finishing second for the second season in a row. Arnold felt like it was time for a change and Manchester United came calling. Arnold was now 31, so he thought a move to Old Trafford would be his last chance to play for such a big club. His first season was certainly a success and, playing to his trademark style, he used his wand of a left foot to dazzle opponents and burst the net. The most significant of his United goals was a penalty scored in the 1983 FA Cup Final replay win over Brighton. Ron Atkinson was his manager at Manchester United, a stark contrast to Robson.

The team were famous for their drinking culture and it was certainly a different environment for Arnold to fully settle. He is remembered by Old Trafford fans as a fantastic player and spent three seasons with the club before he got a call from an old friend. Manchester United would not, after all, be his last chance at a big club. He was now 35 and, when he wasn't even named in the matchday squad for the 1985 FA Cup Final, his career appeared to be winding down. However, Johan Cruyff was back at Ajax, this time as manager, and he called on Arnold. Cruyff remembered the great qualities Mühren had shown during their time playing together and had also seen just how great he had became during his time in England.

Mühren's spell back at Ajax would see him complete the set of European trophies when they won the now-defunct Cup Winners' Cup. Ajax beat Lokomotive Leipzig with

Mühren the elder statesman in a young side featuring Marco van Basten, Frank Rijkaard and Dennis Bergkamp. Mühren insisted he never felt like the father figure of the team. His performances back in his homeland would finally get him the recognition he deserved for the international side. Although the Netherlands had such great depth in terms of quality players, it is criminal that he never made an appearance at a World Cup.

It is such a shame that Arnold was always overlooked and under-rated. However, he would end up having a bigger impact than many who played more internationals once he finally got a run in the squad and was called up for the 1988 European Championship finals. Mühren, as modest as ever, never held a grudge over being overlooked and when that tournament came around, he stepped up to the plate, just as he had done throughout his club career. He was 37 when the tournament began and he played as beautifully as ever, helping or, to word it better, assisting his country to their first major tournament win, as it was from a Mühren cross from which Marco van Basten scored the famous 'impossible' volley that clinched the trophy in a 2-0 win over the Soviet Union.

This triumph meant that Arnold Mühren had won every competition that UEFA had to offer. Bearing in mind that his great assist helped his country win the title, surely Mühren would gloat a little? No chance. 'Everyone said it was the best cross I ever made but that's nonsense. Marco made a not very good pass look very good. Before the ball reached my feet, I saw him running free near the penalty area. If I'd controlled the ball, there would have been another situation, so I decided to play it first time. I was trying to play the ball about two yards in front of him. I thought he would control the ball and bring it back into the penalty area. But he finished it! I've never seen anything like it.'

* * *

A quote from Arnold, found in *Brilliant Orange*, helps us understand the tactical thought process which helped him become so fantastic, a thought process that he certainly shared with brother Gerrie and all the other players who were part of the set-up that would create Total Football. 'It's a thinking game. It's not running around everywhere and just working hard, though of course you have to work hard, too. Every Dutch player wants to control the game. We play the ball from man to man; we wait for openings. That's how to play football; with your brains, not with your feet. You don't have to be a chess player, but you must think ahead. Before I had the ball, I knew exactly what I would do with it. I always knew two or three moves ahead. Before I get the ball, I can already see someone moving in front of me, so when the ball arrives I don't have to think about it. And I don't have to watch the ball because I have the right technique.'

Ajax and then the Dutch national team made Total Football famous. Of course, it did not end there, just as John Tait Robertson's work in England and Hungary has never stopped. Hugo Meisl's work paved the way for every European competition we have today and is constantly being adapted. The culture of football discussion that emerged in the coffee houses of Vienna still exists, even if the venues and situations have changed. The 'Golden Team' of Hungary provided the stage for the game to reach the next level and the Dutch embraced this as the perfect match for their culture, situation and resources.

What happened after that was, of course, for Cruyff to become a manager, create an almost identical, if not better, version of the Ajax 1970s team when he returned as manager in the 1980s and to take his influence on a club to new heights when he built the Barcelona we know today from ideas he learnt growing up within his footballing family at Ajax.

For many fans, Total Football is just one of many different styles of play. To some, Total Football is meaningless and their love for football is just as passionate as that of those who see Total Football as the ideal. The old cliche in football is to go back to the basics. These basics are usually built around man-for-man marking, winning personal battles, keeping the ball out of your own net and building from there. Total Football challenges what the basics are. Jimmy Hogan and John Tait Robertson believed the basics were to pass the ball and move.

Pep Guardiola is perhaps the most famous modern-day advocate of these principles. Although his style of football is not the same as Total Football, he continues to reinvent his style based on old tactics. He most famously played Lionel Messi in the false nine role in a game against Real Madrid. This threw the football world into a frenzy, as many believed Pep had come up with this idea. I'm sure he did, but it was embedded into his subconscious by his footballing father, Cruyff.

Once Michels completed the machine he was putting together, the world of football would never be the same. It was a moment in the history of football when a new chapter began. There is a 'before Total Football' and an 'after Total Football'.

Acknowledgements

THANK YOU to everyone who I have pestered over the years while I have been trying to complete this book. Thank you to my father for trying to understand what I am doing with this book. Thank you to Martí Perarnau and David Winner who, perhaps without knowing it, really helped me get off the starting line with their unrivalled knowledge. Thank you to Jo Araf and Esteban Bekerman for keeping me on the right path when looking at Austria and South America. Thank you to Pitch Publishing for being patient and putting their trust in me.

Cheers, James.

Sources

1. Wilson, J. (2018). *Inverting the Pyramid: The History of Soccer Tactics*. New York, Ny: Nation Books.
2. Wenger, A. (2021). *My Life In Red and White*. S.L.: Weidenfeld & Nicolson.
3. Wilson, J. (2019). *The Names Heard Long Ago*. Kings Road Publishing.
4. Hyne, A. (2019). *Jimmy Hogan: The Greatest Football Coach Ever?*
5. Joy, B. (1959). *Soccer Tactics*.
6. Leatherdale, C. (1996). *The Book of Football: A Complete History and Record of the Association and Rugby Games, 1905–06*. Desert Island Books Limited; First Edition (1 November 1996).
7. Fox, N. (2003). *Prophet Or Traitor?*
8. Meisl, W. (1955). *Soccer Revolution*.
9. Perarnau, P. (2016). *Pep Guardiola: The Evolution*. Edinburgh: Arena Sport.
10. Smith, R. (2017). *Mister*. Simon & Schuster Ltd.
11. Barend, F and van Dorp, H. (1999). *Ajax, Barcelona, Cruyff*. Bloomsbury Publishing.
12. Török Ferenc. *Mandula* (Nyik-ki Bt., 1999)
13. Araf, J. (2021). *Generazione Wunderteam*. Pitvch Publishing.

14. Claussen, D. (2006). *Béla Guttmann.*

15. Bliss, D. (2014). *Erbstein: The Triumph and Tragedy of Football's Forgotten Pioneer.* Blizzard Media Ltd.

16. Campomar, A. (n.d.). *¡Golazo!: A History of Latin American Football.*

17. Kuper, S. (2003). *Ajax, The Dutch, The War: Football in Europe During the Second World War.* London: Orion.

18. Kok, A. (2023). *Johan Cruyff: Always on the Attack.*

19. Cruyff, J. (2016). *My Turn: The Autobiography.* Pan Macmillan.

20. Jones, T. (2019). *Ultra: The Underworld of Italian Football.* London: Head Of Zeus, An Apollo Book.

21. Foot, J. (2006). *Calcio.* HarperPerennial.

22. Winner, D. (2012). *Brilliant Orange.* A&C Black.

23. Bergkamp, D. and Winner, D. (2013). *Stillness and Speed: My Story.* London: Simon & Schuster UK Ltd.